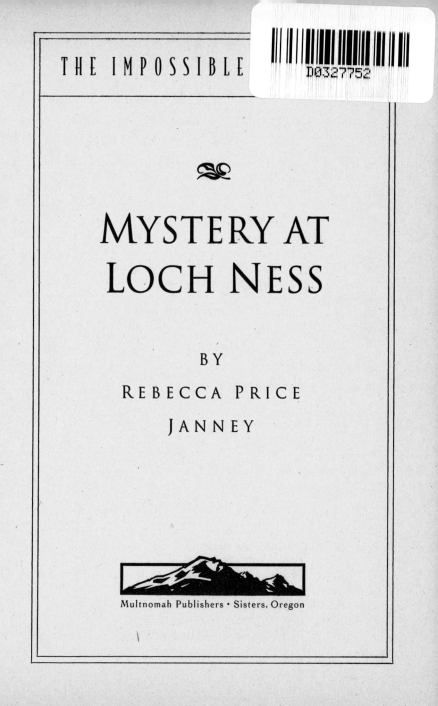

MYSTERY AT LOCH NESS

BY

REBECCA PRICE
JANNEY

Multnomah Publishers • Sisters, Oregon

MYSTERY AT LOCH NESS
published by Multnomah Fiction
a division of Multnomah Publishers, Inc.

© 1997 by Rebecca Price Janney
International Standard Book Number: 1-57673-019-0

Cover illustration by Tony Meers
Design by D^2 DesignWorks

Printed in the United States of America

For information:
MULTNOMAH PUBLISHERS, INC.
POST OFFICE BOX 1720
SISTERS, OREGON 97759

Library of Congress Cataloging-in-Publication Data:
Janney, Rebecca Price, 1957- The Mystery of Loch Ness/by Rebecca Price
Janney. p. cm.–(Impossible dreamers series; bk. 2) Summary: While visiting the virtual reality Lock Ness monster exhibit at a nauticus museum, a
group of Christian home school students travels back in time to Scotland
and to 1934.   ISBN 1-57673-019-0 (alk. paper)   [1. Loch Ness monster–Fiction. 2. Time travel–Fiction. 3. Virtual reality–Fiction. 4. Christian
life–Fiction.] I. Title. II. Series:Janney, Rebecca Price, 1957-
Impossible dreamers series; bk. 2.
PZ7.J2433My 1997 97-26215   [Fic]–dc 21   CIP   AC
        97 98 99 00 01 02 03 — 10 9 8 7 6 5 4 3 2 1

For my mother, Helen Perio,
who encouraged an impossible dreamer.
And to Mary Ann Knox,
my spiritual sister who keeps me inspired.

Chapter One

So, T.J., do you think the monster's real?"

Lindsey Skillman's eyes lit up as her redheaded teacher spoke about Scotland's legendary Loch Ness Monster. At thirteen, she loved mysteries, and this one was a doozy—an ancient sea monster terrorizing people down through the centuries.

"The people the monster's eaten think so!" her brother, Andrew, said.

"No one knows exactly what it is, though," said Lindsey. "A lot of people doubt there is such a thing."

"I'm not sure myself," T.J. replied. "As you said, no one really knows. It's baffled people for hundreds of years. I've always been interested in the Loch Ness Monster, though."

"What's a Loch Ness, anyway?" Andrew was a year and a half younger than Lindsey. He also had a learning disability, which made him slower than Lindsey to catch on to things.

"It's a Scottish lake," T.J. said. "And a mysterious one, too." He pointed to it on a large map.

The school Lindsey, Andrew, and their cousin Ben Tyler attended was a large room in the Skillmans' old house in Williamsburg, Virginia. With desks, chairs, and a blackboard, it looked like any other classroom.

In her eagerness, Lindsey leaned so far forward in her seat that the desk tipped.

"I think the whole idea's stupid," twelve-year-old Ben said. "No one believes in monsters anymore."

Lindsey stared at him. Normally her cousin was positive and fun to be around. Lately, though, she'd found him negative and dull, and she wondered what was bothering him. She decided to ask later. For now she was too wrapped up in the monster legend.

"So where can I get more information about the Loch Ness Monster?" she asked. "Do you have any books about it? I'd love to know if it's for real."

T.J. rubbed his chin. "You know, I think the Nauticus Maritime Museum is running a virtual reality exhibit about it over in Norfolk. It was in the weekend paper."

"Really? Oh, wow! It must be a sign that we should go!"

In her excitement, Lindsey and her desk pitched forward. T.J. quickly reached out his long, strong arm and pushed it back. Unfazed by her near-accident, Lindsey ignored Andrew's and Ben's loud groans. Instead she launched into a hundred-mile-an-hour speech about why they should go to Nauticus.

"Norfolk's so close. I think it's only forty miles from here. We could go to Nauticus for an outside activity trip. Mom and Dad say we need to do stuff like that since you homeschool us, T.J., and we don't get to hang around other kids that much. Besides, we haven't done a field trip yet." Suddenly she gave a loud laugh that ended in a snort. "Unless you count our visit to the Lost Colony!"

T.J. grinned, and Andrew and Ben burst out laughing.

"I'd like to see Nauticus, too," Andrew said. "One of my friends from Little League went there two weeks ago. He said they have a shark and stingray pool, and you can actually touch them. You really like sharks, Ben."

His cousin nodded.

"Did your friend see the Loch Ness exhibit?" Lindsey asked.

"I think so. He said something about going to the bottom of a lake and saving eggs or something."

This sealed it for Lindsey. "We have to go, T.J."

She started leaning forward again, but T.J.'s sharp expression stopped her. She quickly sat up straight and continued. "We could go on Martin Luther King Day. Maybe my friend Sarah can go with us then because all the public schools have that day off. I think we should have the day off, too."

Lindsey had met Sarah Sleeth in her gymnastics class and immediately liked the vivacious brunette. Whenever the girls got together, they talked nonstop, even while shoving handfuls of caramel popcorn into their mouths.

The boys rolled their eyes at her. "That's all we need!" they said in unison.

"You and Sarah are trouble with a capital *T*," Andrew said teasingly.

"I think that's a good idea, Lindsey," T.J. said. "I'll have to check with your folks, though." He paused. "Remember, I can't drive."

Thomas Jefferson Wakesnoris, a direct descendant of President Jefferson, had a condition called narcolepsy. He would fall asleep anywhere and at any time. As a result, he couldn't drive or teach at a regular school.

When her parents and her aunt, Mary Ann Tyler, had decided to homeschool Lindsey, Andrew, and Ben, they hired T.J., whom they knew from church. What they didn't know was that when the twenty-four-year-old teacher concentrated really hard on a history lesson and fell asleep at the same time, he could travel back to that particular place and time.

Once, shortly after he'd started teaching them, he fell asleep during a class about the Lost Colony. When the children tried to wake him up, they found themselves on Roanoke Island in 1587.

Since that adventure, Lindsey had anticipated that something like that might happen again. Now she found herself thinking that maybe—just maybe—T.J. could get her to Scotland to solve the Loch Ness Monster mystery.

After school that day Lindsey was happy to learn that Aunt Mary Ann would be off for a few days over the holiday. When Lindsey asked, her aunt agreed to take her and the others to the Nauticus museum.

"May my friend Sarah come, too?" Lindsey asked her aunt on the phone.

"I don't see why not."

Lindsey quickly hung up and called her friend.

"Your new braces certainly haven't slowed you down, Lindsey." Her father grinned at her as he entered the kitchen and poured himself a cup of coffee.

Lindsey started to huff, but then Sarah answered the phone, and she launched into her invitation. "Will your dad let you go with us?" Lindsey asked moments later.

"Oh, that's no problem at all. He lets me do whatever I want." It was settled.

On the day of the field trip, heavy storm clouds unleashed a furious snow squall with flakes as big as quarters. Lindsey knew her aunt hated driving in snow but begged her to take them to Norfolk anyway.

"The weatherman says it will end soon," Lindsey pleaded. "It'll be okay. Please say you'll go."

Aunt Mary Ann finally yielded. Once they got on Interstate 64, however, traffic moved as slowly as a watched pot boils. The windshield wipers made a rhythmic slip-slap as the mini-van crawled along.

"Can you believe this?" Lindsey moaned. "I'll be a senior in high school by the time we get to Nauticus!"

"I've never seen Route 64 this backed up before." Sarah whistled long and low.

Lindsey's aunt cranked up the radio when the traffic report came on. T.J. had already fallen asleep, as he often did on car trips.

"There's heavy volume on I-64 just before the Waterside Drive Exit at 264 West," the traffic reporter said. "Use extra caution, and give yourself plenty of time."

Sarah elbowed Lindsey.

"What?"

Just then T.J. snorted.

"Listen to him!" Sarah burst into giggles.

Lindsey grinned. Her teacher's condition still amused her at times.

Sarah sang the *Twilight Zone* theme under her breath.

Just then Lindsey spotted a car sliding toward them on the slick road. "Watch out!" she cried.

Chapter Two

Aunt Mary Ann carefully applied the brakes as a piercing horn blasted from the other car. Lindsey lurched forward, but her seat belt kept her from slamming into the seat in front of her.

The minivan coasted about thirty feet, then gently bumped into the guardrail on the side of the road before coming to a stop.

T.J. awakened with a start. "What's happening?"

"W-we almost c-cracked up," Aunt Mary Ann said, her teeth chattering. Glancing into the rearview mirror, she asked, "Is everyone okay back there?"

"We're fine," they said together.

"Boy, that was close!" said Lindsey. Her palms felt sweaty.

The car that had almost hit them pulled in front of the minivan on the side. A middle-aged man in a suit got out and asked Aunt Mary Ann if everyone was all right.

"I'm so sorry," he said. "My car went into a skid on that ice, and I was afraid of plowing into you. I sounded the horn as a warning."

"That's okay," Aunt Mary Ann said.

T.J. had gotten out to inspect the vehicle.

"The front fender's a little scratched from hitting the guardrail, but that's it," he said.

"Thank goodness," Aunt Mary Ann sighed.

Soon they were back on the road again. As the snow stopped falling, traffic started moving more steadily.

"It's going to be so cool when we get there!" Lindsey bounced in her seat. "I can't wait to see the Loch Ness exhibit and the sharks, too."

The word *sharks* came out with a slur because of her new braces, which annoyed Lindsey, since she liked pronouncing words just right.

Sarah punched Andrew in the arm and sniggered. "Isn't she a riot with those braces?"

Andrew shrugged. "She's okay."

Lindsey smiled gratefully at her brother.

"I just hope the Loch Ness Monster doesn't like yellow nail polish." Andrew grinned. "It might make you its next victim."

Lindsey smirked as if to say, "Aren't you the funny one?"

Andrew might not tease her about stuttering and spitting through her braces, but it was open season on yellow nail polish.

"What's wrong with yellow polish? I'm wearing it, too." Sarah jabbed Andrew again.

"Quit that!" He rubbed his arm. Like Lindsey, Sarah was short. Unlike Lindsey, Sarah was sturdy and hit hard.

"Just think of going to the bottom of Loch Ness," Lindsey said. "Somehow they make you feel like you're really there. I read about it in the Nauticus brochure T.J. showed me. You've really been looking forward to that, haven't you, Ben?"

He gave her a half nod. In the front seat his mother had just said something that T.J. was now laughing at. Ben frowned at them.

So that's what was bugging Ben! He must not like how well

his mother and T.J. were getting along. Lindsey didn't think he should worry about it, though. Her aunt hadn't been a widow for very long. Besides, she was too old for T.J. Sarah's father, however, was a different story.

Two hours earlier when Sarah had first met Aunt Mary Ann, she had blurted, "You're pretty! You ought to get together with my dad." Although Lindsey's aunt had laughed, Ben had looked angry about the comment. Sarah might be looking for a new mom, but it was obvious Ben wasn't looking for a new father.

Lindsey thought it was really sad that Mrs. Sleeth had run out on Sarah when her friend was barely two. Since then Sarah's father had kept busy managing a chain of shoe stores, while a series of housekeepers had more or less looked after Sarah. She usually did whatever she pleased, though. Lindsey longed to tell Sarah about faith in Jesus, how the Lord could bring real happiness into her life. She found it difficult, though. How could she introduce her to Jesus without being pushy?

A few minutes later Aunt Mary Ann pulled the red minivan into the Nauticus parking lot. Lindsey, Sarah, Ben, and Andrew joined other excited kids as they spilled out of an assortment of vehicles.

Lindsey became even more animated as they approached Nauticus. Naval vessels, pleasure boats, and fishing craft floated gracefully past the science museum on Norfolk Harbor.

"Wow!" she said. "What a neat-looking place!"

Sarah nodded. "It looks just like a battleship. C'mon, Ben, quit poking around or we'll never get inside."

Ben glared at her.

"Are you all right, hon?" his mother asked. She reached out

to put her hand on his shoulder.

"I'm fine." Ben shoved his hands more deeply into his pockets. He obviously wasn't fine. Lindsey knew she'd have to make time to tell him he was worried about getting a new dad for nothing.

Inside Nauticus, the place was a mob scene. It reminded Lindsey of the song, "The Twelve Days of Christmas." But instead of lords a-leaping, there were children leaping—and dancing and drumming and running and screaming and crying. Someone with a stroller bumped into her, and she tripped over Ben's foot. Videos blared. Loudspeakers made announcements. Lindsey didn't care, though. She only had eyes for the Loch Ness exhibit.

"Let's go there first," she pleaded.

"That's fine with me," her aunt said.

The line for "Virtual Adventures," the Loch Ness show, crawled. Lindsey could barely stand the wait and kept shushing everyone so she could hear the welcoming video. Although it ran three times while they stood in line, Lindsey only caught snatches of the words and picture.

She sighed. "T.J., can you tell what they're saying?"

At well over six feet tall, he had an advantage. "They're talking about the monster as if it's real," he said in his soft Virginia accent. "We're going to be getting into a pod of some sort." He tilted his head toward the video several yards away to hear it better. "Then you put on 3-D glasses." He paused again, looking deeply interested. "Then we'll try to rescue Nessie's eggs from sea monsters and bring them back for scientific research."

"So Nessie's good and the sea monsters are bad?"

T.J. nodded. "That seems to be the case, Lindsey. I think this is really fascinating."

"Seems stupid to me." Ben folded his arms across his chest. "I'd rather see the sharks."

"Don't you want to do this?" Lindsey asked.

He shrugged. Just then the line started moving, and one of the four pods in the Loch Ness adventure opened up. It looked like a carnival ride, and Lindsey couldn't wait for it to start. A Nauticus employee, a teenager with frizzy hair and lots of earrings, stepped in front of them.

"Only five people can go in each pod," she said.

"Bummer!" Lindsey said. "If we squeeze in really hard, can we take six?"

"No way." The employee shook her head.

"Mom, let's go to the shark pool," Ben said hopefully.

Lindsey figured Ben probably didn't want his mother anywhere near T.J. in that little pod.

"You go ahead, honey," his mother said. "You know I get claustrophobic."

Minus Aunt Mary Ann, they all squeezed into the pod.

"I feel like a lima bean." Sarah giggled.

The employee handed each of them a bright orange pair of 3-D glasses. "One of you will be the navigator of a mini-sub," she told them.

Lindsey raised her hand. "I will!"

"And one of you will fire at the sea monsters."

"That would be me," Sarah said.

"Andrew? Ben? Is that all right with y'all?" T.J. asked.

"Sure," Andrew said.

Ben shrugged. He was doing a lot of shrugging.

Then the door closed, and it became dark. Someone pinched Lindsey's knee, and she cried out. "Sarah! Quit that!"

"Quit what?" she asked innocently.

"Ladies," T.J. said sternly. He usually didn't have to say or do much to quiet his students. T.J. just had that way about him.

"You are about to embark on an important mission," a deep voice said while a screen inside the pod lit up and showed them descending to the bottom of Loch Ness.

"It's so realistic," Lindsey said. "Look at all the neat fish!"

"Sea monsters are on the lookout for Nessie's eggs," the narrator continued. "It is up to you to rescue them."

"Look!" Lindsey shouted. "There's a sea monster."

"My ears!" Andrew stuck his fingers in them.

Sarah started shooting wildly at the monster as it approached. "Don't steer me right into it, Lindsey!"

"This is tough." Lindsey struggled with the joystick. "I can't get the hang of it. T.J., would you…"

But T.J. had nodded off.

"There he goes again." Sarah whistled. "I'd better wake him up before you take us right into this monster's mouth."

"Don't touch him!" Ben shouted.

Sarah shot him a look. "Why not?" Before he could answer, Sarah started to shake T.J.'s shoulder. "Hey, what's that? My hand's tingling. Now my arm feels weird!"

Ben tried to pull Sarah away, but it was too late. "Andrew!" he yelled. "Lindsey! It's happening again!"

Lindsey was beside herself. "Oh, wow! T.J.'s time traveling again!"

"Not that!" Andrew cried. He retrieved a mitten from his

jacket pocket and started pulling at Ben.

Lindsey watched as her friend, brother, and cousin entered T.J.'s dream state. Then, placing both hands on T.J.'s head, she yelled, "Don't go without me!"

Chapter Three

A noise like ten thunderstorms rang in Lindsey's ears as she pitched head over heels. "Whoa!" she screamed. Suddenly she landed in a fragrant, though spiny, bush. She waited for the dust to settle so she could tell where she was and what had become of the others. Then someone coughed.

"W-who is that?" she asked.

"Lindsey?"

She tried to answer but choked on a lungful of dust.

"Ben?" asked the same voice.

"Over here," Ben called.

"Lindsey?"

"Is that you, Andrew?" Lindsey hacked. She waved at the dust cloud to clear her vision, and her right hand bumped into her brother's shoulder. "Ouch!"

"My hand hurts, too," Andrew said.

Lindsey rubbed her hand. "Just like last time."

Anyone who grabbed onto T.J., or someone else who was touching him as he time traveled, was rewarded with sore hands for several minutes afterward. Although she was sweeping cobwebs from her brain, Lindsey's heart raced.

She heard more coughing and sputtering as she sat up. She sniffed a clean, smoky fragrance that pierced the odor of the dust. "What smells so good?"

"Beats me," Andrew rasped.

As the grayish dust vanished, Lindsey gaped at the scene before her. From her seat on a purplish bush, she found herself surrounded by large rocks. A lovely clear sky the color of blueberry punch framed rugged mountain peaks. A huge lake glistened several yards away and stretched all the way to the mountainous horizon. Water trickled like fairy fountains from the sides of the hills. The lush green of mossy grass was so bright that Lindsey shielded her eyes.

The sun took the edge off the cool dampness in the air, a good thing since Lindsey no longer wore her Thinsulate parka. She shivered from the chill and exhilaration. As she looked up, she saw Andrew and Ben scattered like clouds over a mound of brush and stone rubble a few yards away. Sarah snoozed loudly next to T.J., who was starting to wake up.

"Hey, kids, are y'all all right?" He rubbed some dust out of his green eyes.

"I'm fine," Lindsey said.

Ben glanced about nervously. "H-have we time traveled again?"

T.J. nodded. "Yes, and Ben, this time you're wearing your glasses, except they're really old-fashioned."

He touched a finger to his nose. "I hate this."

Ben hadn't left his bad attitude behind, and neither had Lindsey shed her braces. Her tongue slid over the uncomfortable appliance, but she quickly forgot about it when she looked at their strange clothes. "Look! We're all in wool pants. And these are the ugliest leather shoes I've ever seen."

"That backpack is pretty weird-looking, too." Andrew pointed at a brown leather satchel with several pockets that lay between him and Lindsey.

Just then Lindsey noticed a camera hanging around her neck. She had no idea how it had gotten there. Of course, when it came to time travel, nothing should come as a surprise.

"Hey, what's going on here?" Sarah demanded, brushing the dust from her pants. "How come we're not in that pod thing? And why am I wearing this stupid outfit?"

"If I'm not mistaken," T.J. tried to explain, "virtual reality has become just plain reality."

Lindsey jumped up and scrambled over the rocks to T.J. She was so thrilled she ignored Sarah's dismay. "T.J., have we gone to Loch Ness in Scotland? Please, please say we have!"

"I think so," he said. "Just before I fell asleep, I was thinking really hard about the monster legend." He glanced around. "Yes, we're definitely in the Highland region."

"How do you know?"

"I studied in Scotland for a semester during college," he said. "Loch Ness is in the Highlands. I'd say that's where we are."

"What are you talking about, T.J.?" Sarah cried. "Loch Ness, Scotland? How can—"

"What year?" Lindsey asked. "It can't be our time because these clothes are too old-fashioned." She pulled at her baggy trousers.

T.J. studied their outfits. Unlike the rest of them, he wore long pants, but the outdoor style of his slacks and shirt was the same. "It's a little hard to tell," he admitted. "Y'all are wearing what appear to be 1930s styles, though."

"Cool!" Lindsey exclaimed. "I'm so excited! Now we'll find out if there really is a Loch Ness Monster."

Sarah frowned. "Will someone please tell me what's going on?"

"What smells so strong?" Andrew poked at the bristly bush he was sitting on.

"That would be Scottish heather," T.J. said.

"I demand to know what's happening." Sarah stomped her foot.

Lindsey was about to explain T.J.'s gift, but just then a short, stocky man walked over to them. He wore a sweat- and dirt-encrusted tweed jacket, and his coal-black eyes flashed angrily.

"And what d'ye think ye be doin'?" His accent was as thick as Lindsey's wool slacks. "It's dangerous to be here."

"We…we…" she stammered.

"We indeed! I niver saw the likes o' ye. There's few people who lives in these parts. What would ye be doin' takin' an outing when we be dynamitin' all around? Ye cud've been blasted to the highest heavens! That, or eaten alive."

"What are you blasting, and who's eating whom?" Lindsey asked uneasily, wondering if her grammar was correct.

The man lifted his cap and scratched a head covered with curly black hair. "As if ye dinna know!"

"We don't," Lindsey said simply.

"We be makin' way for the A82."

"What's the A82?" Andrew asked.

"Why, I niver! And the speech o' ye! I niver heerd an accent like that." He searched their faces. "It's the fancy new road they be callin' a highway. It'll connect Glasgow with Inverness. If we ever git it finished!"

"So, we really are in Scotland!" Lindsey said dreamily.

"And where else would ye be?" asked the astonished man.

"Would somebody please tell me what's going on?" Sarah

asked indignantly. "Why are we in Scotland and not back in Virginia?"

"Later, Sarah," Lindsey pleaded. "I promise, I'll tell you everything later."

"What year is this?" Sarah asked the road worker.

His broad mouth dropped open. "Ye are more strange than sightings of the monster!"

"The monster?" Lindsey asked breathlessly. "Would that be the Loch Ness Monster?"

"Have you ivver?" He threw up his hands and appealed to heaven. "Look here, lassies, this would be April in the year of our Lord 1934. I'm Angus McLeod. We be at Loch Ness, and His Majesty George V's government is springin' for this new road. And it'll take him to finish it at the rate we're goin'!"

Sarah nudged T.J. "Is he speaking English?"

"Scottish." He grinned.

Suddenly a piercing scream rent the air. It was so sharp that Lindsey half expected the sky to tear apart.

"Wh-what was that?" Ben asked with wide eyes.

"I think it was a scream," Sarah answered sarcastically.

"Hey, Angus!" someone yelled. "Hurry, man!"

Lindsey looked in the direction of the urgent voice. Several dozen men in workers uniforms milled around, talking fast.

"I'm a-comin'!" the man named Angus called over his shoulder.

"Please, where are we, Lindsey?" Sarah begged. "What's that weird guy saying? Why does my hand hurt so much, and how come I'm in these stupid clothes? If you don't tell me, I'll scream."

"You heard the man." Lindsey laughed, clasping her

friend's shoulder. "We're at Loch Ness, Scotland, in 1934. I do believe we're about to find out if there really is a monster here."

Sarah's mouth gaped. "You're serious?"

"Look, I told you I'd explain everything later."

"You don't seem a bit surprised!" Sarah exclaimed.

"I'm not. Trust me."

"Famous last words," Ben murmured.

"Well, be quick about it!" Angus's co-worker hollered. "Someone's seen the beastie again!"

Angus's dark eyes shone. "The beastie?" he asked in a hushed tone. "Someone else has seen Nessie?" He suddenly took off.

"C'mon, y'all, let's go!" Lindsey grabbed T.J.'s sleeve, and they began running after Angus.

At the scene, Lindsey and her fellow Impossible Dreamers went unnoticed at first. Several men, talking loudly and all at once, were trying to tell their supervisor, a youthful, barrel-chested man, what they had seen. A dozen reporters clamored to take down every word. Some shouted questions. "What did you see?" "Were you in danger?"

"Please, be quiet!" cried the overseer. "One man at a time, please!"

A reporter elbowed past Lindsey, and she glared at him.

"I saw the beastie cross the road right in front o' me, Mr. Barrie," an older man said. "I come to within three feet o' it, I did! It was just like that woman saw last week. Remember that picture she took, what was in the paper?"

"I seen it, too!" another worker added. "It was long and had humps. I feared for me life!"

"What color was it?" a reporter asked.

The supervisor, Mr. Barrie, waved his hands to try to slow the men's excited chatter. "So you saw something strange—again," he said in a loud, sarcastic voice. "I'm glad you've lived to tell about it. Now, men, we have a road to build. Get back to work."

Out of the corner of her eye Lindsey saw Angus McLeod standing by the lakeside intently watching something. What it was, she didn't know at first. Then a long, dark object thrust out of the water just a few yards from the man.

"Mr. McLeod!" Lindsey screamed in horror as the object drew closer to him. She started running toward him as he turned and ran from the creature. If only she could get a picture of the beast! Lindsey reached for the camera but just then Angus caught up to her and grasped her by the shoulders.

"Did ye see it? Did ye see the beastie?" he asked, breathless.

"Yes, I did," she said.

"I saw it comin' and…"

Angus kept talking, but just then, Lindsey watched in amazement as a middle-aged man of average height and weight ran out of the woods near the water's edge. He charged right up to the creature, blocking her view of it. Moments later, right before he disappeared into the nearby woods, the man caught Lindsey's eye and scowled at her. Then both he and the beast were gone.

Before Lindsey could reflect on what had happened, road workers and reporters pressed in on her and Angus. Her companions also hurried up.

"What happened?" Sarah asked.

"What's wrong?" Ben said.

Mr. Barrie interrupted any further questions. "Now what's

wrong, Angus?" he asked.

"Well, Mr. Barrie, sir, I just saw Nessie."

Barrie's eyes narrowed. "Whatever are you talking about, Angus McLeod?"

"What did Nessie look like?" a journalist asked, pushing closer to the worker. A number of cameras started clicking.

Angus lifted his chin importantly. "She was as big as three men and had a long neck, like a giraffe."

"Did Nessie attack you?" asked a reporter.

"Indeed," he said. "Nessie tried to send me back to my Maker."

Chapter Four

The workers' and reporters' excited voices roared in Lindsey's ears. They were almost as loud as the earlier dynamite blast. Lindsey threw herself into the fray before T.J. could hold her back.

"Mr. McLeod!" she shouted above the din.

But loud reporters surrounded the man, and after several unsuccessful attempts to get his attention, Lindsey resorted to grabbing his sleeve and jerking really hard.

"Hey!" he said, sputtering. "What? What?"

"Mr. McLeod, could you tell me what you saw?"

Startled, he stared at her. "Now what in the world is a wee lassie like you doin' here?"

The other men also stopped talking when they saw Lindsey and her companions. They seemed as surprised as if they'd seen the beastie itself.

She rose to the challenge, throwing back her shoulders and standing straighter. "I want to learn more about the monster."

"But that's ridiculous!" Mr. Barrie walked over to Lindsey.

"No, it isn't," she replied calmly. "I'm here with my, uh, family." She was surprised by her own words, but they just seemed to come naturally.

T.J. approached then, followed by Andrew, Ben, and Sarah.

"I assume you're the father." Mr. Barrie said to T.J.

Their teacher didn't answer one way or the other. Lindsey didn't want T.J. to lie, but it would probably make things easier for them if he said yes. In their previous adventure at the Lost Colony, T.J. had assumed this role. Now, however, they had added another family member, Sarah, who stood there looking baffled and upset.

Apparently Mr. Barrie took T.J.'s silence as a yes. "And what are you doing in these parts?" he asked harshly.

"We're sight-seeing. My family and I are interested in finding out for ourselves about the Loch Ness Monster."

"Yes, I'm hoping to photograph him." Lindsey pointed to her camera for effect.

Sarah started to say something, but Lindsey was close enough to clap her hand over her friend's mouth. She warned her with her eyes, and for once Sarah stayed quiet.

Mr. Barrie sighed. "Yes, the sightings have been more frequent lately. They've really set me back, too."

"How do you mean?" Lindsey asked.

Mr. Barrie inhaled sharply, and Lindsey saw the cords in his thick neck throb. "After five so-called monster sightings last week and two more pictures in the papers, thirty-two of my men walked off the work site."

"We be disturbin' the beastie," Angus McLeod announced. "That's what's wrong. It's all this blastin'. It's got Nessie howlin' mad, I say. We're all in danger. No job is worth losin' yer life for it!"

"Enough of that, McLeod!" Mr. Barrie looked absolutely furious.

The other workers drew closer to Lindsey and her "family," each eager to tell his version of what he'd seen. Reporters started scribbling notes.

"All right, all right!" Mr. Barrie interrupted them. "I'm giving you men a fifteen-minute break. When that ends, it's back to work."

Lindsey felt the press of the crowd as the road workers reported what they had seen. Andrew and Sarah seemed interested in hearing more, but Ben brooded in the background.

"It was real long, about seven feet," said one worker, clearly shaken. "It had humps, too. It moved really slow at first, then took off. I've seen it three times now."

"How many humps?" asked a plump reporter, who wrote quickly.

"Three," the worker answered.

"No, it was four," a coworker corrected him.

"I'm tellin' ye, it was three," the first insisted.

Lindsey's pulse raced. What a thrill to be part of this amazing adventure.

"Did you see its head?" T.J. asked, distracting the workers from their disagreement over the number of humps on the monster.

Several workers nodded eagerly. "It had a small one, compared with the rest of its body," said one.

"Yeah, and it was on a long, skinny neck," another added.

"And its teeth were sharp, like nails," crowed an old, grizzled man. "Its claws was like a dragon's. I jest escaped bein' torn in two by them." A sun ray bounced off a gold tooth.

With his wild gray hair, the man reminded Lindsey of a long ago prophet. In spite of herself, she laughed out loud, drawing some dirty looks. She wanted to believe everything the men were saying, but this man's descriptions were ridiculous.

"Ye think Robbie Ross is lyin', do ye?" He unleashed his fury on Lindsey.

She took two steps back. The monster may or may not have had claws like a dragon, but this guy's breath was on fire. He obviously drank too much. Right then and there she dismissed what he had said.

But Robbie Ross was insistent. "I'm tellin' ye, lassie, the beastie was like somethin' out o' the last Judgment. Just like it says in the Book of Revelation."

"What's he talking about?" Sarah, who had inched closer to Lindsey, whispered in her friend's ear.

"It's in the Bible."

Sarah shrugged. "I've never read it."

"Never ever?" Lindsey asked in disbelief.

"Never ever ever."

"Well, Mr. Ross is referring to a story at the end of the New Testament. It's about God judging the earth, just before history ends."

Sarah waved a hand. "I don't believe that stuff." She stared at Lindsey. "Don't tell me you do?"

"I believe the Bible."

Sarah rolled her eyes heavenward. "We need to talk."

"Yes," Lindsey said, nodding, "we do." She just had to tell Sarah about Jesus. But now was not the time. Three men had shoved Robbie Ross out of the way and were now providing their own description of the beastie.

"So," one reporter said when the men had finished, "it was about five to six feet long, had three humps, a long neck, small head, and was smooth, not scaly?"

"That's right," two men said.

"And it didn't attack anyone?" Lindsey asked.

The men shook their heads in spite of Robbie Ross's loud protests.

"But we didn't exactly stick around to find out if it would or not," a teenager about Lindsey's age spoke up.

"That's right, Johnnie," a man twice his age agreed.

"How much blasting have you done today?" Lindsey asked.

"Just two this morning."

Lindsey's stomach started to rumble just then. What time was it? She glanced at her wrist watch. It wasn't the one she normally wore at home, the one with the cartoon character. This was a plain silver field watch with a brown leather band. Sunlight glinted off the crystal as she checked the hour; it was 8:15 A.M.

"All right men!" hollered Mr. Barrie. "That's enough! Back to work, everyone. Enough of this nonsense. You reporters must go now."

Only a few workers walked away. All the others stayed put. In the background Lindsey heard the low, persistent roar of a motorboat and watched it as it chugged toward the shore.

"What's wrong?" Lindsey said, turning back to the workers. "Why aren't they going back to work?"

"Obviously Mr. Barrie doesn't believe us," the boy named Johnnie answered. "We might be in real danger."

"You know," another man spoke in a hushed voice to Lindsey, "the beastie ate a fisherman a few weeks back."

"What?" she gasped.

Two reporters scoffed. "Oh, that's old news," one of them said in disgust. "No one even knows whether it's true."

"It is too true." The man's eyes flashed. "He was fishin' over by the castle ruins. Up comes Nessie, knocks over the boat, and eats the man."

"D-did anyone find his body?" Lindsey asked.

"Definitely not." He crossed his arms over his chest and shook his head. "The lake never gives up its dead."

Lindsey became as suspicious of this man's story as most of the other journalists, who had trudged off. "How do you know this happened, if the man was never seen again?"

"Are you a doubter?" he asked angrily.

"I think you need to go on more than hearsay," Lindsey said.

"I'll listen!" one young reporter said and gave Lindsey a soft shove.

"Hey!" she yelled. "Don't do that!"

"Yeah, she's my friend," Sarah said huffily.

He ignored the girls. "So, tell me about this fisherman," he said.

"There was no fisherman eaten by the monster," Mr. Barrie said loudly. "It's nothing more than a rumor. Every ethical reporter knows that already. And there is no danger because there is no monster."

"If only you had seen him, sir," Johnnie said.

"Well, I didn't, and I have a road to build." Mr. Barrie was getting testier by the minute. "Do you men want to be out of work again?"

"Sir, sir!" Angus McLeod suddenly yelled from near the shore.

Lindsey turned toward Angus McLeod and another worker, who were walking quickly toward Mr. Barrie. A handsome, middle-aged man in fishing clothes followed slightly behind them. His cabin cruiser was anchored along the shore. Lindsey stood on tip-toes for a better look as another murmur rose up like swirling smoke from the crowd of workers and reporters.

"What is it now?" Mr. Barrie said impatiently.

"He saw the beastie, too!" Angus's companion motioned to the man in fishing clothes.

"Mr. Barrie, this here is Dr. Guthrie MacRae," Angus McLeod said.

The supervisor paid attention. "Yes, I know the reverend." He shook Dr. MacRae's hand. "Catch any fish today, did you?"

"Just a few mackerel," said the newcomer.

The man looked more like a fisherman than a minister. He wore rubber boots to his knees, a brownish-green wool coat, tan wool slacks, and an olive-colored cap with a short brim. The pastor's dark brown hair stuck out at various points from under a tweed cap, giving him a bushy appearance. His angular face was ruddy from exposure to the sun and the Highland wind. Lindsey guessed that Dr. MacRae was at least as tall as T.J. The minister was even thinner than her lanky teacher, though, and at least ten years older.

"What's all this about your seeing a monster?" Mr. Barrie grunted. "Surely you don't go along with this rubbish."

Dr. MacRae's chiseled face broke into a pleasant grin. "I said nothing about a monster. But yes, I did spot something unusual."

The road supervisor's eyes narrowed. "Which was?"

"What did you see, Reverend?" a reporter called out.

The pastor hesitated. Then he said, "I was out fishing in my boat when I heard the last of your blasts. When the dust settled, a three-humped object rose from the lake at the shore-line. It went into the area where some men were working but just as quickly returned to the water."

Mr. Barrie's eyes widened. "Did you see it attack anyone?"

Dr. MacRae shook his head. "That I did not. I did hear screams, though."

"So did we!" Lindsey piped up.

Mr. Barrie shook his head impatiently. "That was just one of my men. He got excited and let out a yell."

"Yes, and there was a strange man," said another worker. "He hung about the edges of the loch and just stared at us, like some apparition."

Lindsey became instantly drawn to this part of the story. She listened closely to hear more but was disappointed at how little there was.

"That's ridiculous," Mr. Barrie scoffed.

"Actually..." the pastor began.

"Enough, men!" Mr. Barrie clapped his hands several times. "Back to work!"

Just then the minister smiled at Lindsey and walked over to her. "Hello, Lindsey."

Lindsey looked at him in surprise. But of course. The same thing had happened at the Lost Colony where she, T.J., and the boys simply fit in as if they'd always lived there.

Sarah's mouth dropped open. "H-how d-does he know—"

"Hello, Dr. MacRae," Lindsey said quickly and as normally as possible, cutting her off.

"Oh, and there you are, T.J." The pastor shook T.J.'s hand as the road workers stared in astonishment.

"So, you see, Mr. Barrie, we weren't lyin' to ye," said Angus.

"The good minister here saw it, too."

"But he didn't see a monster." Mr. Barrie rolled his eyes heavenward.

"Call it what you will, sir. I still say it's a monster, and we're in no small danger. What about that fisherman who was killed the—"

"Well, Dr. MacRae, I appreciate your report," Mr. Barrie said, interrupting the man's speech. "But it's time my men went back to work. Be careful on the loch. We'll be doing more blasting this week."

"I will."

"Come along, men!" Mr. Barrie shouted.

The men reluctantly obeyed. Lindsey heard them murmuring about quitting as they returned to their road-building duties. Within minutes she and her fellow Impossible Dreamers were alone once again, except for the minister.

"Well, I do believe Mary has prepared a little breakfast for us." Dr. MacRae broke into a grin. "We don't want to keep her waiting, do we?"

Lindsey glanced at T.J. for guidance. He winked at her, then said, "No, we certainly don't."

"Good. Let's be off then!"

Just as Lindsey turned to go, she heard a rustling in the woods near the shore. A wild-looking man stood staring at them. Before she could point him out to the others, however, he fled.

Chapter Five

Lindsey smiled as she lifted her face to the morning sun and felt the spray from the fishing boat's wake. The wind tousled her hair and caused her to feel a bit chilled. She could see T.J. up front in the small cabin talking with the pastor.

"I'm glad someone's enjoying herself." Ben folded his thick arms across his chest.

"I am!" she exclaimed. "Just think, we're right here on Loch Ness. How many other people get to check out a mystery this closely?" She found herself scanning the lake for signs of the monster she had seen earlier.

"Well, it makes me nervous."

"Are you okay, Ben?" Andrew looked worried. "You haven't been yourself today."

For a moment, their cousin's attitude softened. "Oh, I'll be all right. I guess I'm just having a bad day."

Lindsey remembered how angry Andrew had been during much of the Lost Colony adventure. He kept saying how badly he wanted to have T.J. fired. But he didn't seem to mind being at Loch Ness at all. He seemed even peaceful, if not as excited as Lindsey.

"I'm sort of glad we're here," Andrew said.

"Are you nuts or something?" Ben shook his head.

"No," he said slowly. "It's just that if I have to learn history,

I'd rather do it like this." He grinned. "It's a lot easier for me than reading a book."

Andrew suffered from dyslexia, which made him confuse numbers and letters.

"Yeah, well, it won't be if we don't get back," Ben said.

"We got back the last time, Ben," Lindsey reminded him.

"Just barely," he muttered. "How do we know we'll make it again? I feel like a time bomb about to go off."

"Ben, I think I know what's bothering you, and—"

Lindsey was cut off by Sarah, who suddenly grabbed her arm. "Lindsey Skillman, if you don't tell me what's going on, I'll push you overboard!"

Lindsey laughed. "Okay, okay!"

"Why are we in Loch Ness? How did we get here?"

"Shhh!" Ben hissed, putting a finger to his lips. "Dr. MacRae will hear you."

"I don't think he can," Lindsey said. "That motor is so loud."

"So what if he hears us?" said Sarah.

"We can't let him know we're from another time," Lindsey explained. "T.J. told us that if our true identities were known, people would want to know the future so they could change it. We're just here to find out what happened."

Sarah gaped at her friend. "I think you're all nuts! What in the world are you talking about?"

"Better start from the beginning," Andrew said.

"Okay," said Lindsey, "you know how T.J. falls asleep so easily?"

"Yeah."

"Well, sometimes he really gets into a lesson he's teaching us."

"Especially history," Andrew said.

"Yeah, and when the history lesson has a mystery in it and then he falls asleep," Lindsey explained, "T.J. goes back to the place and time he was thinking about."

Sarah listened quietly as Lindsey described T.J.'s strange abilities.

"When he first started teaching us at home," she went on, "we didn't know he could time travel. So when T.J. fell asleep after telling us about the Lost Colony at Roanoke Island, he just sat there in a trance. When we tried to wake him up, we got stuck on him."

"Just like in the pod at Nauticus!" Sarah cried. "I felt all pins-and-needles and like I was getting sucked into something."

"Yep." Lindsey nodded. "So here we are because T.J. was thinking so hard about the Loch Ness Monster today."

"I wonder why we're in the 1930s, though," Andrew said.

Ben remained quiet, staring moodily into the distance.

"I'm not real sure," Lindsey said, watching her cousin out of the corner of her eye. "It could have something to do with that road they're constructing."

"That must be it," Sarah said. She seemed to be getting into the spirit of the event. "That video at Nauticus said sightings of the monster increased after the government built a road in the 1930s."

Lindsey frowned. "I couldn't hear the video. It was too noisy in there. What else did it say?"

"I was practically sitting on top of a speaker," Sarah said with a grin. "That was about it." Suddenly she brightened. "Wow! It just hit me, Lindsey! If we're about to solve an unsolved mystery, think of the money we can make!" Her brown eyes shone. "Think of how famous we'll be. Our faces will be plastered all over magazines in supermarkets!"

Lindsey and Andrew exchanged glances. Lindsey had never thought about making money or getting famous off their adventures. She didn't think Andrew had either. It seemed wrong somehow, like telling a stranger your mother's age and weight.

"That's not right, Sarah," Andrew said.

"Why not?" She threw her hands up. "You guys are such goody-goodies! Homeschooling has made you forget what the real world is like."

"Not as long as you're here," Andrew joked.

Lindsey almost burst out laughing, but she held back. Andrew had made his point.

After a few moments Sarah said, "This is too weird. If I'm thirteen in our time, what does that make me in 1934?"

"Thirteen," Lindsey said.

"Strange! So," Sarah said, rubbing her hands together, "how do we get back home anyway?"

"Pretty much the same way we got here," Andrew said.

"It won't happen, though, until the mystery gets solved," Lindsey told her.

Her friend looked a little worried. "How long will that take?"

"We don't know."

"But won't people miss us? What will your mom think, Ben, when we don't come out of that pod?"

"She won't think anything," Ben mumbled over his shoulder.

"When we go back like this, our time stands still," Lindsey explained. "No one knows we're gone or misses us."

"That's really weird." Sarah whistled between her teeth. "So how does that minister know us?"

"That's part of it, too." Lindsey spread her hands. "The people we go back to often know us. We don't always know them, though. It can get tricky. Sarah, when in doubt, don't say a thing." She spoke the last four words slowly, to get her point across.

"Okay," her friend agreed. She paused, then added nervously, "Uh, by the way, is there any chance we won't make it back?"

"I think so," Ben spoke up. "We almost weren't all together when we left the Lost Colony. This is such a nuisance! I don't think T.J. is safe. Maybe he shouldn't be teaching us."

Lindsey looked at Andrew, and they laughed. Andrew had said the same thing during the first trip.

"Ben, that was my line," her brother said. "Give it a chance. You'll be your usual happy self in a little while."

The trip across Loch Ness to the minister's croft took twenty minutes. Lindsey was amazed by the size of the lake; she had had no idea how huge it was. She thrilled to the sights of elegant birches perched like ballerinas near the shore line. A red antlered deer caught her attention once as it sprinted into the woods after a cool drink of water. There were very few dwellings, except for the occasional fisherman's or shepherd's croft.

When they arrived at a simple wooden dock, T.J. helped

Lindsey out of the boat first. The wind had chilled her, and she hugged herself.

"Is that your croft?" she asked the minister, pointing to a lovely cottage on the hill.

The stone building sat back some fifty feet from the shore. It had a pretty flower garden and a white fence. It looked friendly, welcoming.

"Aye," Dr. MacRae said.

"It's bonny!" Lindsey exclaimed.

"Now, where did you pick up that expression?" The minister chuckled.

"Probably from the movies." She felt her face turn red.

Just then the door to the charming croft opened. It framed a tall, beautiful woman and a perky white dog that immediately raced down the hill to its master. Yipping noisily, it threw itself at Dr. MacRae.

"This is our West Highland terrier, Robbie Burns. Burnsey for short," he called over the dog's excited barks.

"Oh, I love dogs!" Lindsey dropped to her knees to pet the pooch.

The Westie leaped at Andrew, who petted him, then at Ben, who patted its head a few times.

"Why Robbie Burns?" asked Andrew. "Is that somebody famous?"

The pastor's jaw dropped. "Surely you know who he was?"

Andrew shook his head. "Sorry."

"Only Scotland's greatest poet!" He turned to T.J. "What do the schools teach American children?"

"We'll be working on poetry next." T.J. grinned.

"I hope so! Well, let's get inside."

Lindsey walked a little unsteadily up the hill toward the gray stone croft with its tightly thatched roof. The motor's roar still echoed in her ears as she struggled to get her land legs back. She surveyed the croft, noting that a newer addition had been added. It was of the same simple style as the original building, but the stones were less worn by time and weather. Lindsey was eager to learn to use her camera so she could take a picture of the house.

Mrs. MacRae greeted them almost as joyfully as her dog; she didn't jump all over them, however.

"Do come in!" she exclaimed, hugging everyone as they entered. Lindsey smelled a clean, sharp fragrance about the cheerful woman. Like her husband, Mrs. MacRae was tall; unlike him, she was elegantly dressed in a tweed suit and high heels. Her nails were painted a maroon color, and her dark blonde hair was fashionably bobbed. She would have looked right at home in the city. Here, she seemed slightly out of place.

"Was everything all right while I was gone?" Dr. MacRae asked, embracing his wife.

She nodded. "Yes, thank God."

"We'll get everything straightened out," he assured her.

What was that all about? Lindsey wondered.

"You must be half-frozen and half-starved," Mrs. MacRae said to her guests. "These mornings on the loch get so chilly. I usually don't go out until at least noon."

Lindsey sniffed many delicious smells wafting together. She couldn't distinguish them, but the aromas made her mouth water. Ben's stomach rumbled loudly, and she suppressed a giggle.

"I made breakfast for us." Their hostess motioned toward

the kitchen and a large table set for seven. The dog suddenly yipped and leaped at her. "Old Burnsey here knows what I've been up to." She laughed. "He can't wait to have some."

A fire glowed in the kitchen, and although the cottage felt damp, the wooden ceiling beams and floors warmed the croft in a different way. Modern paintings graced the walls, and oriental rugs decorated the floors.

"Guthrie, dear, the fire is dying," Mrs. MacRae said to her husband. "Will you stoke it while I show everyone to their rooms?"

"Of course." He smiled at his guests. "I dare not stay out fishing too long in the morning. My wife would freeze."

"He's right. I don't know the first thing about tending a fire." She seemed almost proud of that. "Now come along. I have the two guest rooms made up, boys in one, girls in the other."

They followed Mrs. MacRae across the kitchen and living rooms to the addition. It held three small bedrooms, one for the MacRaes and two for visitors. The guest rooms each had a trundle bed.

"The water closet is across the hall," Mrs. MacRae told them.

"Water closet? What's that, Mrs. MacRae?" Lindsey asked.

"Oh, dear! I suppose you call it something different in America." She lowered her voice. "It's where the toilet and tub are arranged. I told my husband that if we were to vacation in the Highlands, I must have modern conveniences. I couldn't stand to be cooped up in an old shanty." Before Lindsey could respond, she continued, "By the way, your suitcases arrived last night."

"Suitcases?" Lindsey's eyes opened wide. Her joy knew no bounds when she spotted a leather case with the initials "LSW" engraved on it. Inside she found several changes of clothes and a warm-looking sweater. "Thank you, Lord," she whispered, for he could be the only explanation. Back at the Lost Colony, Lindsey had worn two outfits the whole time in blazing hot weather. Now she had several. She loved that about God; he cared about the little things that concerned her. She really needed to talk to Sarah about him.

"I'll give you fifteen minutes to freshen up," Mrs. MacRae told her guests. "I can't hold breakfast longer than that. You'll find extra towels under the sink." She pointed to the bathroom.

"Thank you for your hospitality," T.J. said. "We'll be along shortly."

Mrs. MacRae clapped her hands. "I'm so glad you're here!" Then her voice dropped as she said, "I do miss the city so. Besides, there's safety in numbers."

Chapter Six

Lindsey didn't have time to follow up on Mrs. MacRae's mysterious remark. Her companions looked hungry. Andrew seemed especially eager to eat. Even Burnsey was pawing and begging for his breakfast. After washing up, Lindsey went to the large kitchen where everyone had already crowded around the white cloth-covered table. With a healthy fire burning in the hearth, the croft felt snug and warm. Although her heavy wool sweater itched, she didn't mind too much. At least the chill had gone out of her bones.

"Let us thank the Lord for this food," Dr. MacRae said from his seat at the head of the table.

Lindsey noticed that Sarah didn't bow her head as the pastor prayed.

Mrs. MacRae, who had tied a frilly white apron around her slender waist, got up to serve them. She filled their stoneware mugs with strong, black tea first. Then she ladled hot, buttery porridge—oatmeal to the Americans—into their bowls.

Sarah craned her neck as if looking for something.

"What can we get for you, Sarah?" the minister asked.

"Brown sugar."

"We don't use sugar on our porridge, Sarah, dear," Mrs. MacRae said. "We use salt."

Sarah made a face, which embarrassed Lindsey. She hoped the MacRaes didn't take offense. They didn't know Sarah was growing up without much guidance about manners.

"Is there ketchup?" Andrew asked.

"Ketchup?" Dr. MacRae repeated dumbly.

"Andrew, I think you'll need to get used to not having ketchup on the table," T.J. told him.

Lindsey knew that would be tough. Her brother put ketchup on everything, even oatmeal.

The hot cereal tasted strange at first, but Lindsey quickly grew to enjoy it. The cream was much thicker and tastier than the milk she had at home. She was hungry, and the porridge made her feel so warm that she ate a second bowl.

"That was wonderful, Mrs. MacRae," she said, feeling very satisfied.

"I'm glad you enjoyed it, dear. I hope you'll like this as well."

Lindsey's eyes bugged out at the sight of the enormous platter Mrs. MacRae placed in the middle of the table. It brimmed with so many eggs and so much bacon and sausage that the serving fork on it tottered. Burnsey started to leap at the food, but the minister held him back.

"Wow!" Andrew and Ben exclaimed.

Ben hadn't looked that happy since just before Sarah had tried to fix up their parents. He did love to eat.

He and Andrew dug into the mound of meat. Sarah also approached it enthusiastically. Lindsey knew that Sarah ate mostly TV dinners and sandwiches at home, so this would be a real treat. T.J., who had been to Scotland before, didn't seem at all surprised by the amount of food on the table.

Lindsey wanted to be polite and so she took one of each kind of meat. Then she picked at them with her fork. With Burnsey's upturned face at her knees, she figured out how to move small pieces of meat from her plate to the dog. It was an old trick she'd picked up from a movie, and it worked. Relieved not to be overeating, Lindsey wanted to find out more about Loch Ness and its famous monster.

"How did the monster legend get started, Dr. Mac?"

As soon as his butchered name was out of her mouth, Lindsey gasped. T.J. brought his linen napkin to his mouth, but Sarah and the boys didn't try to mask their laughter.

"That's all right, Lindsey." The minister kindly patted her hand. "I like the sound of 'Dr. Mac.' It makes me feel that you're not afraid of me, the way some children are of ministers."

"Thank you," she muttered. She didn't like being referred to as a child. But the pastor was being so kind, she didn't get too upset about it.

"In fact, all of you may call me Dr. Mac," he told the Dreamers.

"And I will be Mrs. Mac," his wife said.

"Now, then, Lindsey, you asked about the monster legend," Dr. Mac said.

"Yes, I know a little about it, but not when and how it got started."

The friendly minister put down his fork. "You may know that Saint Patrick brought Christianity to Ireland," he said. "Well, Scotland had Saint Columba, who lived in the sixth century."

"I've heard of him," T.J. said. "Wasn't there a book about him?"

"Indeed. It's called *The Latin Life of the Great Saint Columba*. It goes back to 565 A.D. In fact, I might have a copy of it somewhere around here." He gazed toward a bookshelf across the room. "I usually keep some good volumes on hand. I like to read a lot on vacation. Do you, T.J.?"

"Yes, sir, I do," the teacher said.

"I just read an excellent book by Hemingway. Do you like him?"

"Yes," T.J. said as Lindsey became impatient.

"I think he's making quite a name for himself. Now, I also am quite fond of T. S. Eliot. He's become quite the Englishman, too. I think he spends more time in England than in his native America."

"Guthrie, dear," his wife interrupted. "I think Lindsey was asking you about the Loch Ness Monster."

The minister looked befuddled. Then he said, "Yes, yes, of course! I do go off sometimes. Where was I?"

"You were telling us about St. Columba," Lindsey said as Sarah giggled.

"Right! Yes, in one chapter of that book about him it says that the saint arrived in Loch Ness just after a monster had killed a resident."

Lindsey listened raptly. So did the others, even Ben. As the pastor talked, she fed her last piece of bacon to Burnsey. She was sure she'd made a friend for life.

"Columba needed to send one of his companions across the loch," Dr. Mac said, sipping his tea. "The man was terrified, though. The people who lived there warned him not to tempt the monster. But Columba would hear none of it."

He really knew how to tell a story, when he didn't go off on some tangent or other. Lindsey was sure he must preach good sermons.

"As the saint's companion went onto the loch in his wee

boat, the monster approached," Dr. Mac said. "In the book it is called 'the fiercesome beastie.' When it was within ten feet of the man, St. Columba took action. His voice carried across the water, 'Go thou no further nor touch the man. Go back at once!' The startled bystanders watched as the terrified creature fled into the water. The saint's companion made it safely to the other side. As a result, Christianity continued to spread throughout these Highlands."

"That's really interesting." Lindsey leaned forward with her chin on her palms, elbows on the table. Then she realized how rude that must look and straightened up.

"There's another recorded sighting from the 1500s," Dr. Mac said. "It's in a book called *The History of Scotland*. There it says that a terrible creature suddenly came up out of the water and swallowed three men."

Dr. Mac's wife rose from the table then, only to return a few moments later with two Scottish newspapers. "I thought you might want to see photos that have recently appeared in the press." She handed one paper to Lindsey and the other to T.J. "The picture you have was taken by a woman tourist a few weeks ago, Lindsey. And T.J., the one you're holding was snapped by a British physician last week when he passed through the area."

Sarah looked at Lindsey's photo, while the boys peered over T.J.'s shoulder to see the picture in his newspaper.

Lindsey became excited. "This one looks just like what I saw!"

"You saw Nessie?" Mrs. Mac asked.

Lindsey explained what had happened, as the boys pressed closer to the photos.

"I've seen this one in a book," Andrew said when he saw the second photo.

Their hosts looked puzzled. Wincing, Lindsey closed her eyes. *Nice move, little brother.* When she opened her eyes, she saw that Andrew's face was redder than his hair.

"I m-mean, it looks familiar," he stammered.

Just then the minister's wife got up and brought yet another dish to the table. It was big and black and looked like a giant roasted coal.

"Is that a pudding?" T.J. asked.

Mrs. Mac looked pleased. "Yes. It's a spicy black one with haddock."

"Gross!" Sarah exclaimed. When everyone gaped at her, she looked confused. "What? What did I do?"

Lindsey felt like crawling under the table.

"I think you owe Mrs. Mac an apology," T.J. said quietly. "She's gone to a lot of trouble to fix us a nice Scottish breakfast."

"Gee, I'm really sorry, Mrs. Mac," Sarah said. "I didn't mean to hurt your feelings or anything. It's just that I've never seen anything like your, uh, pudding before."

Mrs. Mac didn't seem upset. "Thank you, dear. You don't need to take any of this if you don't want to."

"I do think I'll pass," Sarah said.

Although Lindsey hadn't expressed her opinion out loud, she had to agree with Sarah's view of the pudding. She didn't want to offend her hostess, though, so she took a tiny amount. She could tell that Ben and Andrew weren't too enthused either. They each took only a small spoonful, then picked at it.

Lindsey returned to the discussion. "Do people who

believe in the monster think it's the same one today as in Saint Columba's time?"

Dr. Mac chewed a big bite of hot pudding before answering. He clearly enjoyed it, as did T.J. "Some do. Those would be the more superstitious locals, wouldn't you say, Mary? And by the way, this pudding is delicious."

His wife smiled her thanks. "You're right. No thinking person believes it's the same creature from hundreds of years ago."

"What about the fact of the monster itself?" Lindsey persisted. "You're smart people. Do you believe that what's out there is really a monster?"

The minister and his wife glanced at each other.

"I don't doubt that something unusual is living in the lake." The minister became thoughtful for a moment. "But by 'unusual' I mean something not fully understood. Perhaps the creature is really quite ordinary. But to us who don't know yet what it is, the beastie is a mystery."

His wife nodded. "I doubt it's really a monster at all. Or that it kills people."

"Some road workers claim they've seen the beastie," Dr. Mac said, "and that it actually crossed the road near them."

"Yeah, and it attacked one of them!" Andrew said.

"And one guy told me it ate a fisherman a few weeks ago," Lindsey added.

The minister and his wife chuckled. "I wouldn't put much faith in those reports. The man who claims to have been attacked is often drunk, and we read about the so-called death in the paper last week. It's little more than rumor." He pulled at his chin and stared straight ahead. "Still, I'd like to know more about what's out there."

"Before my husband entered the ministry," his wife said, "he studied biology at the University of Glasgow."

Dr. Mac appeared to be thinking hard. A few moments later he said, "One of my professors had a theory. You see, Loch Ness is one of Great Britain's largest freshwater lakes, as you Americans call lochs. Dr. Kerr thought it was once an arm of the North Sea. She believed some large creatures could have been caught here when the loch and sea were cut off from each other." He paused. "Tell me, T.J., are you interested in monster hunting?"

"Yes, as long as we're here it makes sense to investigate this fascinating legend."

"Well, you can certainly stay busy enough at it. With this new road going in, there have been many reports about the monster. Some of them are far-fetched, but others make sense."

"There are all sorts of ideas about what the beastie is," Mrs. Mac said. "Some say it could be an otter, since they've been spotted at Loch Ness."

"Or maybe a reptile of some sort," her husband added. "Some scientists think it might even be a relative of a long-ago colossal amphibian. I've even read theories about it being a giant worm-like creature. Then there's the idea that the humps people see could simply be gas bubbles rising from the loch's floor." He was on a roll. "It might also be a sturgeon. Those fish can weigh up to five-hundred pounds."

"You're really into this, aren't you?" Lindsey said.

"Yes, I suppose I am. My ancestors came from this area, so it's in my blood, you might say, to be interested in the beastie."

"What do you think it is?" Lindsey asked. "You saw something out there."

"It could've been nothing at all, just shadows. The loch plays funny tricks on the eyes. Still, I'd like to see it again, maybe photograph it. There is something out there, all right."

"You saw the beastie?" his wife said in surprise.

The minister described what he had seen on the loch.

"Oh, Guthrie! Were you afraid?"

"No." He shook his head. "Just fascinated." He paused then asked, "Do you mind if I escort you around, T.J.? I'd love to join your quest for the monster."

"That would be great," T.J. said. "We could use your expertise—and your boat, if you don't mind. You're being very kind to us, especially to house and feed us."

"Nonsense!" he said. "You are our guests. Besides, Mary is chomping at the bit here. She's a city girl, you know."

They smiled lovingly at each other.

"I'm just about finished redecorating the croft," she said. "The garden is the only thing keeping me sane here. I'm thrilled to have company besides my radio." She gestured toward a huge cabinet near the couch. "Half the time I can't get a signal this far out." Then with a grin, she added, "I brought my phonograph, though, and I often play American records. I just love Bing Crosby!"

Sarah scrunched her dark eyes at Lindsey and formed the question "Who?" on her lips.

"A famous singer," Lindsey whispered.

As they went on discussing the monster, Mrs. Mac brought out a heap of toast and a barrel of marmalade.

Lindsey groaned. "I don't think I can eat another bite."

"That's why you're so thin!" Mrs. Mac said.

"I'm afraid we Americans aren't as generous with our

breakfasts as the Scottish are," T.J. said.

Mrs. Mac nodded. "Yes, I went to New York some years ago. I nearly died when I saw the meager breakfast the hotel served. Toast and eggs. Can you imagine!"

"How do you stay so thin and eat like this?" Sarah asked in astonishment.

Lindsey rolled her eyes. Her friend couldn't seem to say anything right this morning.

Mrs. Mac laughed. "Oh, we don't eat like this at every meal. And we have lots of activity."

"How big is Loch Ness?" Lindsey asked, wanting to change the subject.

"Very big," the pastor said. "It's over twenty-five miles long."

"It's only about a mile wide in most places, though," his wife added.

"How deep is it?"

"Something like 750 feet," he answered. "That would be at its deepest. The mean depth is just over 400 feet. It's also very cold, staying at about 42 degrees."

"Brrr!" Lindsey shivered.

"It's not Scotland's biggest lake, though. That would be Loch Lomond. That one is—"

Sarah cut him off. "Why hasn't anyone captured the monster?"

He became thoughtful. "The creature is so sly. The conditions are harsh, too. All year long, sudden gusty winds can appear. We also get a fair share of thick fog and rain. The region we're in, the Highlands, gets the most annual rainfall in Scotland."

"A lot of that is snow," Mrs. Mac said as she presented the last course—a Scottish scone served with strawberry jam and something like whipped cream. There was, of course, a great deal more tea with which to wash it down. In spite of her glutted feeling, Lindsey enjoyed the strong tea. By now, she was feeling nice and warm.

"How long has the road construction been going on?" she asked between sips.

"Several months now," the pastor said. "Part of the A82 is finished."

"I'm glad it's going in," Mrs. Mac said. "It will make our holiday trips here much more convenient. Those dirt roads are so narrow. And when a sheep strays into the road, it's difficult to move on."

"Do you have a car here with you?" Lindsey hadn't remembered seeing one.

"Yes and no," Mrs. Mac said. "We can't get it to the croft. There aren't enough roads, so we keep it at a garage in Inverness. That's the closest town to Loch Ness. It's just a few miles away."

"Who decided to build the road, Dr. Mac?" Andrew asked.

"The government." He lit his pipe before continuing.

Usually Lindsey hated the smell of smoke. She found this aroma pleasant, however.

"The Scottish economy is very depressed. This is a way of upgrading our roads and putting men back to work."

"That's right. Aren't we in the depression of the 1930s?" Ben asked.

Lindsey sighed. There was no end to her fellow Dreamers' reckless questions. She didn't want the MacRaes to become suspicious, after all. For all they knew, the Wakesnorises were just a nice little family traveling through Scotland on vacation.

"Of course we are, Ben," Dr. Mac said. "Many people are out of work. A number of Glaswegians have come to Loch Ness to find work on the road."

"What's a Glaswegian?" Lindsey hoped this wasn't a stupid question.

"A resident of Glasgow," Mrs. Mac explained. "That's where we live when we're not on holiday."

"The city used to be a major center of ship-building," her husband said, puffing on his pipe. "Manufacturing and industry were also its great strengths, as they were for all of Scotland. Now Glasgow has over sixty percent unemployment."

"Wow!" Lindsey exclaimed. "That's amazing."

"That's why it's so important to support projects such as the road building here," he went on. "Poor Peter Barrie. He's afraid even more men will get so afraid of the monster that they'll walk out on him. He's already lost a large number. He can't afford to lose his job either. He's terrified that his children will become like thousands of others living in the gorbals or on the street."

"Poor man." Mrs. Mac shook her head. "I know his wife from church work in Glasgow, where they're from. This is his first job in two years."

"What's a gorbal?" Andrew asked.

"We'd call it a slum in America," T.J. answered.

"Oh."

Suddenly Lindsey remembered the strange man she'd heard the workers talking about at the road construction site. Was he the same one she'd seen along the shore?

"Dr. Mac, a road worker said he saw an odd person hanging around today. Then, just before we got into your boat, I saw someone weird, too. He was big and wild-looking. Do you know anything about him?"

He and his wife exchanged glances. "We've seen him, as well. A big fellow with a mop of white hair?"

Lindsey nodded.

"Who is he?" Andrew asked.

"I don't remember seeing anyone like that," Sarah said.

Mrs. Mac shuddered. "The locals call him the Haunted Highlander."

Chapter Seven

I've seen him up close twice and tried to talk to him," the minister said. "He only walks away, though. He lives in a croft not far from here. I've called on him a few times during my walks, but he's never there."

"Who do you think he is?" Lindsey asked.

"Certainly not a ghost!" the pastor exclaimed. "But we Scottish people love a good ghost story, and sometimes we get carried away. Have you ever heard of the Glen Coe ghosts?"

"No."

"Guthrie, you're getting off the track again," his wife warned.

"Sorry." He gave a laugh. "With me one subject leads naturally to another. At any rate, that mysterious man is not a ghost."

"Sometimes I'm tempted to think he is." Mrs. Mac became somber as she stood over T.J. with a warmed-up teapot. "I mean, considering all the upsetting things that have gone on around here lately."

Lindsey was on red alert. She wasn't sure how the strange man was related to the Loch Ness Monster mystery, but he might be. After all, he was around during the latest sighting, and the locals didn't seem to know much about him.

"Surely you aren't serious about his being a ghost!" The minister didn't seem to appreciate his wife's remark.

"Now, Guthrie, of course I don't believe in ghosts." Mrs. Mac poured another cup of tea for T.J., then sat down. "At least not the way superstitious people do."

"I don't understand." Sarah spoke up. "Either there are real ghosts or there aren't."

"Not exactly." Dr. Mac put down his pipe as Burnsey pawed at his master for attention. He thoughtfully stroked the dog's fuzzy white head. "There is a spiritual part of our world. Do you, for example, believe in angels?"

Sarah shrugged. "I don't know. People talk about them enough, though."

Dr. Mac lifted his dark eyebrows. "They do?"

Lindsey realized that Sarah was referring to their time, not his. "In America they do," Lindsey said, trying to smooth things over. "I think angels take care of God's children."

"Yes, that's part of what they do," the minister agreed. "Well, just as there are angels, there are also demons. Angels do God's work. Demons do the devil's. And sometimes what people claim are ghosts are actually demons at work. Other times, there's a logical reason."

T.J. nodded. "That's what I believe, too."

The other Dreamers, except for Sarah, nodded in agreement. "I'm not so sure there even is a God," she said flippantly.

Lindsey felt sad. She couldn't imagine not believing in God. Maybe Dr. Mac would think of something to say that would open Sarah's heart. Surely a minister would be good at leading someone to Christ.

"Why not, Sarah?" Mrs. Mac asked tenderly.

"I just don't know how to believe in something I can't see."

"That's difficult for a lot of people," the minister said.

Neither he nor his wife seemed at all shocked by Sarah's doubts. "Do you believe in oxygen?"

Sarah nodded. "Of course."

"You can't see it, though, can you?"

"No, but I can breathe it."

"How about love?"

"No, but I can feel it—well, sometimes." Then she grinned a little. "I think I see what you're getting at."

"Believing in God and following him is the most wonderful thing in life," Mrs. Mac said. "Feel free to ask us any questions you might have."

"She's right," her husband said kindly. "Just remember, Sarah—seeing isn't always believing."

"Except when it comes to Nessie!" Lindsey laughed.

"Yes, except when it comes to Nessie," the pastor repeated.

Lindsey waited for the minister or his wife to press Sarah to make a commitment to Christ. But they didn't, and she wondered why. Maybe they didn't think Sarah was ready yet. Lindsey really didn't know much about sharing her faith, but she was willing to learn how to do it.

After a few quiet moments, Lindsey turned to the pastor's wife. "A few minutes ago you said something about weird things happening here. What did you mean?"

Before his wife could respond, Dr. Mac said, "The rock blasting for the road has been a nuisance. Dust over everything—that bothers her more than it does me, of course." His eyes twinkled. "Loud noises. Being rudely awakened early in the morning. The dog barking because his ears hurt."

As if to underscore his comments, another blast rocked the

area. Dishes in the cupboard rattled, while glasses and cups on the table did a little jig. Burnsey leaped toward the front door and started barking.

"Just like that." The minister looked sheepish. "So much for a peaceful vacation. They're supposed to be finished with that part of the road construction. Unfortunately, the monster sightings and walk-outs have put them behind schedule."

Mrs. Mac shook her head. "The blasting is annoying, but that's not all that's upsetting me."

"What else has happened?" Lindsey asked as Dr. Mac went after the barking dog. He brought Burnsey back to the table and put him on his lap.

"When we first arrived, I put Burnsey outside while I cleaned the croft," Mrs. Mac said. "He was on his leash, and I tied him to a small tree trunk. Fifteen minutes later, he wandered into the house! He wasn't wearing his leash or collar."

"Could he have slipped out of them?" Andrew asked.

"I suppose. It's just that I couldn't find them anywhere." She spread her long, pretty hands for emphasis. They reminded Lindsey of her Aunt Mary Ann's artistic hands.

"Another time I noticed that the front door was wide open," she continued. "It shuts very tightly, though. It wasn't even windy that day."

"Yes, and someone tampered with my boat," Dr. Mac added. "I couldn't get the motor started. When I looked more closely, I saw all the petrol was gone."

"Petrol?" Ben asked.

"Gas," said T.J.

Lindsey was glad to see her cousin joining in the conversation.

He seemed to be in a better mood.

"He had just filled the tank," Mrs. Mac said. "There weren't any leaks either."

"Several times peat and firewood have been stolen, too."

"Peat is something Scottish people use to build fires," T.J. told the Dreamers.

"What or who do you think is behind these things?" Lindsey asked.

"We don't know. I think it might possibly have something to do with the mystery man we talked about earlier. It's certainly not a ghost!" Dr. Mac laughed.

"Maybe we can help you find out," Lindsey offered. "Maybe this is all tied up with the monster mystery."

"Thank you, Lindsey," Mrs. Mac said. "We don't want you to worry about staying here. No one and nothing has been hurt."

"Not yet anyway!" Sarah said.

Lindsey shook her head in amusement. "Sarah, you have a way of saying just the right thing."

Sarah gave a little bow as the others chuckled.

"Speaking of things we don't understand," Dr. Mac said. "That brings us back to the beastie. T.J., how long will you be here, and what's on your list of things to do today?"

"We aren't exactly sure on either count," he answered. "I hope that isn't a problem for you."

"Not at all!" Mrs. Mac said. "As I said, I love company. I get so lonely out here."

"Thank you, Mrs. Mac. That's very kind," T.J. said. "As for today, I'd like to explore the loch." He turned to the others. "How about the rest of you?"

"That would be great!" Lindsey said, and Andrew and Sarah agreed. "Maybe we could talk to some of those road workers again."

"Exploring the loch is easily enough done, but Peter Barrie might not let you near his workers," Dr. Mac said. "Anyway, I'll be glad to take you on a tour in the boat." He put Burnsey down and slapped his palms against his thighs. "Well, then, let's get ready to explore! Mary, are you coming?"

"I don't think so, dear. I'd like to clean up around here first."

"You can always get back to it later."

"You know me. I'd rather not get all cold and wind-blown."

"I'll help you here," Ben said suddenly.

"Oh, my dear, you go along. There's so much to see. You don't want to miss out."

"I'm pretty tired of traveling today." Ben looked at his teacher. "If you don't mind, I'd really rather stay here."

T.J. hesitated for a moment. "If you like, you may stay," he said finally.

"I would like that."

"Well, I won't turn you down if you insist, Ben." Mrs. Mac smiled at him. "It'll be nice to have the company, and I really don't want to go out on the loch today. It's a bit nippy for me."

"Let's get ourselves in order then." Her husband rose. "Be sure to wear jackets. The weather is cool this time of year." He glanced at his watch. "We'll meet in fifteen minutes at the boat."

"Yes, and I'll prepare a picnic lunch for you to take," Mrs. Mac said.

"I don't think I'll be able to eat for at least a month," Sarah told Lindsey on the way to their room.

"It was overwhelming," Lindsey agreed.

T.J. intercepted them in the hallway after they got past the MacRaes. "You know that one newspaper photo of the monster?" he asked.

"The one I nearly spilled the beans over?" Andrew said.

T.J. cuffed him lightly on the back of the neck and laughed. "That's the one."

"It's really famous," Lindsey said. "I've seen it a lot of times in books."

"Yes, well, the man who took it died in 1994. Before he passed away, he admitted it was a hoax."

"Really?" Lindsey exclaimed.

"Yes. He and a few fellows put together a pretend monster and took a picture of it."

"I wonder if the guy I saw at the same time I saw Nessie could have been part of the hoax," she said. "Something didn't seem right."

"So there is no monster, then?" Sarah seemed disappointed.

T.J. shrugged. "Who knows whether that other picture was the real thing. Just because one was a hoax doesn't mean they all are."

"That's what we're here to find out!" Lindsey said cheerfully.

The trip around majestic Loch Ness took the entire day. The lake was huge, and the MacRaes lived roughly mid-way on the beautiful loch, on the western side.

Lindsey nearly wore herself out looking for the monster.

Every time she saw something the least bit odd, she pointed and yelled, "Look! I see something!" Before long Andrew and Sarah were imitating her. That didn't stop her, though. Lindsey was determined to be the first to spot Nessie. Dr. Mac showed her how to use her camera when she confessed it was new to her. Soon she was snapping pictures, wondering if they'd ever be developed or if she'd be back home by the time they were.

"We aren't far from the Urquhart Castle ruins," Dr. Mac announced at one point. "First, however, I'll take you south."

There the minister showed them the tiny village of Fort Augustus.

"The fortress was built in 1715," he said. "After falling into disrepair, most of it was demolished in the 1870s."

"It looks pretty good now," Lindsey said.

"Benedictine monks built an abbey there," he said. "They also run a very good school. They take good care of the property."

"Do they ever see the Loch Ness Monster?" asked Andrew.

"There have been a few sightings," Dr. Mac said. "Normally, though, Nessie seems to lurk in the northern part of the loch."

He skillfully guided the motorboat northward as Lindsey gasped over the gorgeous scenery. The tall mountains inspired her complete awe. So did the vibrant green of the grass that sloped toward the lake. The air fairly snapped with freshness as Lindsey inhaled deeply. With a heavy wool sweater and sturdy jacket, she was able to enjoy the refreshing wind. It kissed her face and played with her hair. Apparently Sarah was enjoying herself as well.

"Isn't this great?" Sarah's cheeks glowed, and she was smiling.

"It sure is," Lindsey said. "I'm glad you're getting into the spirit of being here."

"Yep! And I'm especially thinking of all the fame and fortune that's going to come our way because of this."

"Oh, I hope not, " Lindsey said. "It would spoil everything to share this adventure with just anyone." Some things just weren't meant to be shared, but she didn't know how to explain it to her friend.

Around lunchtime everyone started mentioning the picnic basket Mrs. Mac had packed for them. At breakfast Lindsey had thought she'd never be hungry again. But after being in the fresh air for two hours, she was. Dr. Mac was so excited about showing them the loch, however, that he moored the boat near Urquhart Castle and trudged them around for the greater part of an hour.

"The castle was originally made of wood," he told them.

"When was it built?" Andrew asked.

"In the twelfth century."

"My gosh!" Sarah exclaimed. "In Williamsburg people fuss because something's a couple hundred years old."

When the minister raised his eyebrows in a puzzled expression, Lindsey intervened. "We live in an old town back home in the United States," she said. She knew that Colonial Williamsburg wasn't fully restored by 1934.

"Oh, I see." Then he went back to his speech about the castle ruins. "Anyway, two hundred or so years later, stone walls replaced the wooden structure," he said. "In the late 1600s a fire destroyed the castle. This is what's left."

Dr. Mac then showed them to an especially scenic spot where they lunched on oat cakes, cheese, and tea from a thermos. Across the lake they could see some road-building activity. The equipment and men looked quite small from a distance. Lindsey took a few pictures from this vantage point.

During the course of lunch, she reached out to touch a tiny purple flower. "Ouch!" she cried, quickly withdrawing her hand. A tiny drop of blood trickled from her palm. T.J. handed her a clean handkerchief to cleanse it. A closer look revealed the prickly leaves circling the flower.

"That's a thistle," he told her. "I believe it's Scotland's national flower."

"That's right," the minister said. "It's a very sturdy flower. Difficult to uproot. In the 1200s the Scots were able to fend off a nasty Norwegian invasion because an enemy soldier stepped on one of those thistles and cried out in pain. It gave away their position to the Scots, saving the day."

"I believe it!" Lindsey cried. "That really hurt." Then she asked, "How far is Inverness? Does the loch go all the way to the city?"

"Yes, there's a three-mile section of canal that joins the two."

After lunch they explored that area, then headed south on the opposite side. They eventually came to the road construction area where all was far from well. Peter Barrie was in an even worse mood. A number of machines and equipment lay idle, and a lot fewer men were around. After the supervisor finished barking at some of the workers, T.J. approached him. Lindsey lingered nearby with her camera, ready to take a picture of Nessie should he make another appearance. The others stayed farther back. Lindsey figured they weren't too keen on getting in the irate man's way. She wasn't particularly worried about that. She just wanted to learn more about the Loch Ness Monster.

"What's happened, Mr. Barrie?" T.J. asked.

"Oh, this blasted monster business has my men in a panic," he said.

"Did they see it again?"

"So they say. More of them have walked off. Just like that!" He snapped his strong fingers, making a loud pop. He glowered at Lindsey as he heard the click of her camera, so she let it dangle from her neck once more. "Others are threatening to leave. I'll never complete this road!"

"Do you think they'll be back?" T.J. asked.

"Who knows?" Mr. Barrie threw his hands up. "Now there's a rumor about an ancient curse."

"What kind of curse?" Lindsey asked.

"Some garbage about how digging up the road will bring a curse on those who do it. It's pure nonsense, but some of the men think this so-called monster is the curse and that if they keep working on the road, they'll die."

Chapter Eight

Lindsey was especially curious to know more about the curse. She strongly suspected it was the result of a rumor. But who had started it?

"I'd love to talk to some of the workers," she told Dr. Mac and the other Dreamers after they left Peter Barrie.

Dr. Mac said that most of them had come to Loch Ness from Inverness, Glasgow, and Edinburgh. They all stayed at various inexpensive road houses or inns at Inverness.

"Even if they've walked off the job," he said, "those from far away probably wouldn't head for home this late in the day."

"So they still may be at Inverness?" Lindsey asked.

"I should think we can find some there, if you want to go," he said. "If you think it will help you learn more about the beastie."

"Oh, I do want to go!" Lindsey cried. "It will help. I'm sure of it." Then she remembered that T.J. was in charge of her, Andrew, and Ben when their parents weren't around. And in this case, of Sarah as well. "Is that all right, T.J.?" she asked meekly.

"Sure, that is if you don't mind, Dr. Mac. I'd like to know more about this myself."

"Me, too!" said Andrew.

"Me, three!" Sarah chimed in.

"I don't mind at all," Dr. Mac said. "I'm just as eager as any-one else to solve this great mystery of the centuries. We can take my boat through the Caledonian Canal to the town. Inverness isn't very big. We can walk or take a bus once we get there—or we can get my car if that would work better. There's just one thing, though." He paused. "We'd better go back to the croft first. I don't want Mary and Ben to worry about us. I also don't like to leave her alone too much with all these strange happenings. Besides, she loves going into Inverness to shop. It makes her feel less isolated."

"Why do you stay at the croft if Mrs. Mac doesn't like it?" Sarah asked bluntly.

The minister laughed. "Sarah, indeed you are an original! Little do you know how many ballets and operas I endure throughout the year for the sake of my dear wife."

"Oh," she said, blushing. "Sorry."

"That's all right. In a good marriage, there must be compro-mise."

When they arrived at the croft, Lindsey hurried up the stone path first. Burnsey's greeting was to jump all over her.

"Goodness, Lindsey, what has you so excited?" asked Mrs. Mac. "You look as though you've seen Nessie again."

"Unfortunately, I haven't," she said, kneeling to pet the excited Westie. Her cousin came into view then, looking more settled than earlier in the day. "Hi, Ben."

"Hi, Lindsey. What's up?"

The others joined them as Lindsey relayed all that had happened. "We're going into Inverness to find and interview some workers," she concluded.

"Would you like to go, dear?" Dr. Mac asked his wife. "Ben,

you're welcome, too, of course. I thought all of us could go along."

"Oh, I'd love to!" The tall woman clapped her hands in childlike delight. "When do we leave?"

"As soon as you can get yourself ready."

Mrs. Mac headed for the croft while pulling off her white apron. "I only need to run a comb through my hair and put on some lipstick," she called over her shoulder.

"I'll go, too," Ben said, then to Lindsey he whispered, "It can get pretty boring here. I can understand why Mrs. Mac gets excited about company and going into town."

Fifteen minutes later the whole lot of them piled into the boat, Burnsey included. They reached Inverness just as it was getting dark. Dr. Mac moored his boat and asked an attendant at the dock if he knew where the road workers were staying. It couldn't be a very big place if the dock hand could answer that question.

"They would be on the east side o' the river," he told them proudly. "On Castle Road there be several boarding houses. Ye'll find most o' the men stayin' in them." He poked Dr. Mac in the ribs and laughed in a raspy voice. "Unless they be in the public houses!"

The minister thanked the bearded man and turned to his wife and guests. "We should take a bus. It may be quicker than if we get our car on the west side of the river."

They walked to a bus stop a few blocks away.

"How big is Inverness?" Lindsey asked as they waited at the bus stop.

"I'd say about thirty thousand." Dr. Mac looked at his wife for confirmation, and she nodded.

Lindsey was startled. "But that man knew so much about what was going on that I thought it must be a much smaller town."

"I can understand why you would think so," he replied. "That dock man is famous for knowing other people's business."

"Which river runs through Inverness?" T.J. asked.

"The River Ness."

"What's a public house?" Ben asked innocently.

The minister cleared his throat, and his wife giggled.

"Some of them are English-style pubs," T.J. began, "where families can go to eat and play board games or darts, for example. Others are less, shall we say, family-friendly."

"The one that dock guy mentioned sounded like the last kind." Sarah chuckled.

"If that's what it's like," Mrs. Mac said, "the girls and I can go to a nice restaurant and do some shopping."

"Could I get a kilt to take home?" Sarah asked eagerly.

"I don't see why not," the pastor's wife said.

Lindsey started to explain that you can't take things with you when you time travel, but then she remembered that the MacRaes didn't know their whole story. "I need to tell you something about that later," she whispered to her friend.

Soon a red double-decker bus swung into view. Lindsey insisted on sitting up top, though it was more crowded. From there she had a great view of the charming town with its centuries-old streets and buildings in gray tones. Sarah liked it, too.

"This is so cool," she said, as she sat down next to Lindsey. "I can't wait to tell everyone back home."

Lindsey sighed. "That's what worries me."

"Y'all have been hoarding your experiences." Sarah sounded a bit angry, Lindsey thought. "You need to share this with the world." Then she muttered just loud enough for Lindsey to hear, "I've always wanted to be on a talk show."

Lindsey found herself praying that God would help Sarah understand that some things are too special to share with just anyone at any time. She thought about the Bible story in which Jesus took Peter, James, and John up on the mountain. There Jesus' clothes became a dazzling white, and his face shone like the sun. He also talked to Moses and Elijah, who appeared before them. But then Jesus told his friends not to tell anyone what they had seen until after he rose from the dead.

Lindsey wanted God to show Sarah that this trip was about more than appearing on talk shows and getting rich from it. She hoped that in the course of finding out the truth about the Loch Ness Monster, Sarah would also discover the truth about God and his Son, Jesus.

"What are you doing, Lindsey?" Sarah asked.

"Praying."

"Well, don't. It makes me nervous." Sarah crossed her arms and turned her back on Lindsey. She quickly got absorbed in the sights passing by outside the window.

The group visited only one boarding house before finding out where the road workers were staying. A middle-aged woman with a scarf tied over her head pointed to another large house down the street. "There ye'll find some of the men," she said.

But they weren't in. They were having one last fling before returning home, beyond the reaches of the horrible Nessie.

"I guess Dr. Mac and I will need to go after them," T.J. said.

"And leave us out?" Lindsey protested.

"You can't go into a place like that." He pointed toward a rowdy public house a few doors away.

"We can go someplace nice, Lindsey." Mrs. Mac's voice both coaxed and soothed. "I can show you a nicer part of town."

"How about if you go get some men and bring them to us, to a nice place?" Lindsey suggested, holding her ground.

The minister and T.J. thought they could manage that. Mrs. Mac felt differently, though.

"Can't they just tell you about the men?" she asked Lindsey.

"They could, but I'd so like to hear their stories myself," Lindsey insisted politely but firmly.

T.J. agreed to bring some men to Lindsey and the others, if Mrs. Mac didn't mind. Although she admitted she didn't understand it, she relented. Dr. Mac told them to wait for him and T.J. at a nice hotel a block and a half away. Mrs. Mac then took them all there, and they waited in the pleasantly-furnished lobby. The road workers, seeming eager to tell their stories, showed up with the pastor and T.J. some fifteen minutes later.

"I can't promise how reliable they are," T.J. whispered to Lindsey. "They've been in the pub for quite a while."

He proved correct. The eight men who came to tell their stories about the monster sightings and curse rumor went into great detail about red and green dragon-monsters who ate bulldozers whole. There was a great deal of knee-slapping and loud laughter. Several times Mrs. Mac openly worried that the hotel manager might throw them out if the men didn't quiet down.

On top of that, some journalists appeared, egging the workers on for more information, creating a festive atmosphere.

When one worker bumped recklessly into a tall, expensive-looking vase, Dr. Mac tried to send the men back to their boarding houses. "All right, men, thank you for coming," he said, waving at them to get their attention.

It didn't really matter. Lindsey could see there was no true story there anyway.

"You may go now, men." T.J. pushed each of them toward the door, and the men filed out, stumbling over each other. The journalists left as well.

Then Lindsey saw a familiar-looking young man come through the door. When he saw her, he walked toward her. The other Dreamers and Mrs. Mac were too busy helping Dr. Mac and T.J. shepherd the unruly flock to notice.

"I saw you at the road site today," he said.

"Yes. Your name is Johnnie, right?" When he nodded she asked, "What are you doing here?"

"I heard of reporters being here," the tall boy said, "listening to the stories about Nessie. I wanted to set the record straight."

Lindsey could tell he was sober and wanted to talk. He also struck her as being better educated than the men with whom he worked. She led him to a nearby overstuffed chair and sat opposite him.

"So, what's really going on out there?" she asked eagerly.

"I'm not exactly sure," he said. "It's just that one of the reporters has been real friendly with a man who came today to help Mr. Barrie."

"What man?"

"I think his name's Barbour. He's with the government, too. Mr. Barrie didn't introduce him to us yet, so I'm not sure what he's doing. Anyway," he said, his blue eyes flashing, "I saw Barbour hanging around with a reporter from the *British Mirror*. They whispered a lot to each other."

"What's the reporter's name?" Lindsey asked.

"Uh, I think it's Campbell."

"What do these men look like?"

"Barbour is middle-aged," Johnnie said. "He has grayish brown hair, a mustache, and he wears glasses."

"How tall is he?"

"Oh, maybe five feet nine."

"And Campbell? Can you describe him?"

"Sure. He's a bit younger and a little taller. He's much heavier, though. He has thinning brown hair with some gray in it and also a mustache."

Lindsey made a mental note of these descriptions. Barbour sounded like the man she had seen run up after she'd spotted Nessie this morning. "What do you think is going on?" she asked.

Johnnie shook his head. "I don't know. They just seemed pretty suspicious to me, real secretive."

"This is really interesting."

He nodded. "By the way," he said suddenly, "I don't know your name. I'm Johnnie, of course, and my last name's Marshall."

She stuck out her hand. "Lindsey Skil—" She stopped abruptly, remembering that she was time traveling as T.J.'s daughter. "Uh, Lindsey Wakesnoris."

"I might try to forget my name, too, if it were Wakesnoris," he teased. When Lindsey frowned, though, Johnnie apologized. "I didn't mean to insult you."

"Thanks." After a pause she said, "Johnnie, I hope I don't offend you by saying this, but you seem more educated than the other workers."

"I suppose I am. You see, I'm a college student at the University of Edinburgh. Or was, that is." He looked sad. "My papa died last year, and most of his insurance was worthless. These are such hard times that I've been working to support my mother and two sisters."

Lindsey didn't know what to say. She'd never had to face poverty in her own life. Finally she simply thanked him. "Will you let me know if you hear anything else?"

"Sure. I guess I'll see you around. I, for one, am not about to quit my job. Money's too scarce for that."

"Hey, Lindsey!" Sarah called as she walked toward them. "We wondered what happened to you." She looked first at Lindsey, then at Johnnie, and grinned slyly. "Well, excuse me!"

Lindsey managed to keep her cool. "This is Johnnie Marshall. He's working on the road. Johnnie, my friend Sarah Sl—, uh, Wakesnoris."

"Your friend has the same last name?" Johnnie asked in surprise.

"We—"

Before Sarah could get another word out, Lindsey slapped her hard on the back. "We're sisters, but I think of her more like a friend."

Johnnie's eyes danced with delight. "Oh, I see."

"Well, we have to go now."

"Nice meeting..."

Lindsey pulled Sarah by the arm and steered her toward their companions.

"Hey, Lindsey, what is this?" Sarah shook her off, then turned to stare hard at her. "You won't let me talk!"

"You keep saying things that could get us in big trouble," Lindsey said but instantly regretted her hasty words. "I'm sorry, Sarah. I guess I'm just feeling a little nervous about people finding out who we are. It's really important that we fit in."

"Why?"

"Because we could mess up the whole process of coming back to solve the mystery about Nessie." Then she added, "We can only go home, you know, when we solve the mystery."

Sarah gulped. "I'll try harder."

"Hurry girls!" Mrs. Mac called to them from the entrance of the hotel's restaurant. "It's time for dinner."

As they headed toward her, Sarah whispered to Lindsey, "It's a wonder she's not as big as Nessie with all she eats."

"Shh!" Lindsey hissed, but she couldn't help giggling.

Dinner was fairly uneventful—until just before they left the restaurant to return to the croft. Two men came and sat down three tables away from them in the fern-filled dining room. They spoke urgently to each other in low tones. Lindsey remembered Johnnie Marshall's description of the shady reporter and government official. It seemed to fit. Could the official be the man she'd seen this morning? If so, what had he been doing?

Just then Dr. Mac laid his linen napkin on the table and announced that it was time to go. "The loch gets cold at night, and we have a distance to travel."

Lindsey was the last one to file out. As she walked, she brushed past the table where the two men were seated. At that moment a waitress carrying a loaded tray approached, and Lindsey dared not budge until waitress and food had safely passed. It was only a moment, but it was long enough for Lindsey to overhear part of the men's conversation.

"So, you're bringing out the big guns, eh?" asked the older, thinner one. "What a press conference that will be!"

His companion nodded. "It's supposed to end the rumors."

"So they think!"

Both of them laughed.

"Excuse me," Lindsey interrupted them. The older one gave a start, as if he recognized her. She clutched her camera. "I've been trying to photograph Nessie," she said. The man's curious expression changed to a suspicious scowl. "I think it would be great to sell my photos to an American newspaper so people there could learn more about the monster. Are you with the press?"

The men rose out of forced politeness. "David Barbour," said the thinner one. "I'm with the Scottish Tourism Bureau."

"Oh, I see. You're not a reporter."

"I am," said the other. "The name's Will Campbell. I'm with the *British Mirror*."

"I'm Lindsey Wakesnoris," she said. "What's this about a press conference?"

"Lindsey, were you eavesdropping?" T.J. stood at her side.

The men's mouths dropped.

"I'm afraid I heard them mention it as I walked by."

Mr. Barbour puffed out his chest. "The Prince of Wales will

be at the road site tomorrow at ten to assure the workers that there's nothing to be afraid of."

"He has his work cut out for him," the reporter snickered.

Chapter Nine

Lindsey couldn't get to sleep that night. On the trip across Loch Ness she had kept her eyes peeled in search of Nessie while the others huddled close around the cabin to stay warm. She was beginning to worry that she might never see the legendary monster again, if indeed there really was one. In addition, Lindsey was excited about seeing the Prince of Wales in the morning. She had begged Dr. Mac to take her to see him, and he had agreed, saying that an opportunity like that didn't often come along.

On top of all those things, Lindsey was worried about the McRaes' safety. Upon returning to the croft, the minister had discovered a broken window. Burnsey barked continually during the resulting investigation, and Lindsey had found a rough stone on the floor inside the croft. Jagged pieces of glass surrounded it.

Her mind full of these things, Lindsey shifted first one way, then another in her bed in a vain attempt to get comfortable. Around four o'clock, she finally fell asleep.

Sarah awakened her at eight. "Everyone's taking turns in the bathroom," she said, toweling her thick hair dry. "You're next."

Lindsey yawned loudly. She wasn't much of a morning person. The thought of meeting the prince and searching for Nessie, however, gave her a reason to get up.

"T.J. says we'll be leaving at nine. Breakfast is in a half hour." Sarah lowered her voice. "I sure hope Mrs. Mac doesn't serve that disgusting pudding again."

"I didn't like it either, Sarah," Lindsey said, becoming worried anew about what Sarah might say or do. "If she does, though, please don't say anything. Mrs. Mac has been so nice to us."

"Yeah, yeah, I know. I promise to behave myself." She bowed low, and Lindsey giggled.

"Am I ever glad there's a bathroom here," Lindsey said a moment later. "You should've been with us at the Lost Colony." She shook her head. "No running water. No bathrooms. No TV or radio. No electricity."

"Sounds rough."

"It was, but I loved being there." Lindsey hugged herself. "What a time we had! And what a time we're having now! We're going to solve the Loch Ness Monster mystery."

Sarah grinned slyly. "And get rich and famous as a result. I already know what house I'm going to buy for me and my dad with all that money. Maybe Ben and his mom will join us."

"Oh, Sarah, don't tease him. Ben's really sensitive about that. Besides, I don't care if we get rich off this!" Lindsey exclaimed. "Just knowing the answers to these mysteries is enough for me."

"Don't be such a futz! You'll change your mind sooner or later."

"I don't think so," Lindsey said firmly.

Fortunately there was no fish pudding for breakfast. But there was plenty of excitement. Lindsey had been photographed seeing Nessie the day before, and her picture had made the papers. Dr. Mac had gone out very early to get the papers at Inverness. Lindsey could hardly concentrate on food.

Everyone set off in the boat at nine o'clock, including a beautifully dressed Mrs. Mac. "I wouldn't miss the chance of seeing the prince!" she told everyone.

"I still say you should have put on warmer clothes and sensible shoes," her husband complained.

"I'm fine, Guthrie," she said.

Lindsey thought she looked stunning in her tweed suit with matching hat and shiny black leather gloves. Her gold-framed sunglasses gave her the look of a model. Suddenly Lindsey had a brainstorm. "Hey! I just thought of something."

"What's that, dear?" Mrs. Mac asked.

"Oh, sorry. I get carried away sometimes. It's just that I remembered something. Isn't your king the grandfather of Princess Elizabeth?"

"Yes, that's right, dear. I see that even American girls follow their royal highnesses." She seemed quite pleased about this.

"There's another one?" Sarah asked.

"Well, at least *some* American girls follow the princesses," Andrew teased. Ben remained quietly in the background, like a piece of furniture.

"Yes, Princess Elizabeth has a younger sister, Margaret Rose," Mrs. Mac explained.

"So, the Prince of Wales is their uncle?" Lindsey guessed at placing these people and their positions. "And he's next in line to the throne?"

"I thought the Prince of Wales was Charles," Sarah said. "You know, Princess Di's ex."

Lindsey rolled her eyes. What would her friend say next? "I'm afraid you're wrong, Sarah," she said. "This prince will be king after His Majesty George V. Then he'll be Edward VIII— and give up his throne for the woman he loves."

Mrs. Mac gasped, and her husband nearly collided with another boat. T.J. gaped, and the boys just looked stumped. Lindsey, realizing the enormity of her goof, tried to backpeddle.

"I, uh, I…" There seemed no way out of this one.

"My gracious, child!" Mrs. Mac exclaimed, staring at her. "Do you have the second sight?"

"The what?"

"Second sight. Many Scots believe some people can see into the future. Some say it's a gift from God, others from the Enemy. I've never given it much thought myself. Until now, that is." She continued to stare at Lindsey, who felt just horrid. After all her fuss about Sarah's goof-ups, she had made a great big one.

"Maybe she can tell us who broke our window!" Dr. Mac joked.

"I…I don't have second sight," Lindsey said. "I guess I just daydream too much. Your prince is so handsome and a bachelor, after all."

This satisfied Mrs. Mac, whose accent became thicker with pride. "Aye, he is at that."

"So, Dr. Mac, do you expect many reporters for this event today?" T.J. asked, changing the subject.

As they discussed the visit, Sarah leaned close to Lindsey. "I'm not the only one putting her foot in her mouth."

"I guess not." Lindsey gazed in embarrassment at the wooden deck. "Sorry."

"Don't worry about it, huh, Linds? Just don't jump down my throat when I goof up."

"I'll try not to."

"Forget it."

They eventually reached the site of the prince's arrival, which was clearly marked by a large crowd of journalists, road workers, and some people from Inverness. Apparently news had traveled quickly. A swarm of reporters buzzed around, waiting for the prince. It took several minutes for Dr. Mac to find a place to dock. Finally, after the minister parked the boat, Lindsey and her companions hurried toward a stage someone had hastily built.

It was a beautiful, crisp day with more than a touch of spring in it. Birds sang, and tiny flowers bloomed underfoot, along with the prickly thistles Lindsey had learned to steer clear of.

"I wonder how so many people found out about this visit," Mrs. Mac said as they pushed closer.

"Yeah, it's not like they have cell ph—ooph!" Sarah cried out as Lindsey poked her in the side.

"What's that?" the minister's wife asked, lifting her sunglasses.

"Oh, nothing." She and Lindsey giggled.

Lindsey was just glad T.J. hadn't heard them.

Ten o'clock came and went. No Prince Edward. Ten-fifteen. Then ten-thirty, and still no prince. Andrew had brought a pack of cards, and he and Ben took turns playing solitaire on a tree stump. Then finally, at ten-forty, a commotion began.

Lindsey jumped up and down to see over the heads of the taller people in front of her.

"There he is!" she shouted as a gorgeous Rolls Royce came into view.

Two agents jumped out of the car and opened the door for the stylish prince.

"Here he comes!" Lindsey cried. Then, frustrated because she couldn't get a good camera angle, she asked T.J. if he would hoist her onto his shoulders. He did, and from that vantage point, Lindsey snapped several pictures of the good-looking prince and the tall, sophisticated woman who was with him. The prince was handsomely groomed and wore a perfectly tailored tweed suit. He was almost boyish-looking, although he had to be at least forty.

His companion wore an elegant wool suit, and her bobbed red hair made her look something like an aging actress. Nevertheless, she was very professional in the way she carried herself. She stayed two paces behind the prince as he shook hands with Peter Barrie and several of the workers. Then the prince and the woman mounted the platform.

"Guthrie!" cried Mrs. Mac. "Isn't that Dr. Kerr?"

The pastor's face broke into a smile when he saw the woman.

"Yes, it is!"

Lindsey wanted to ask him about this Dr. Kerr, but someone called for quiet.

"It is truly a pleasure to be with you today," Prince Edward spoke in a high-pitched, crisp British accent. Lindsey took several pictures of him from her perch on T.J.'s shoulders. "What a lovely place Loch Ness is! This new road, the A82 as it is called, will bring thousands of people here every year to enjoy these Highlands. It is a good project, a noble project. It is necessary for Scotland's future."

He paused and looked around at the crowd. "If only to make it easier for motorists to maneuver around sheep, it is necessary. That is why I am late in joining you."

A ripple of laughter broke out over the spellbound audience. A few people applauded.

"Isn't he handsome?" Mrs. Mac swooned as she craned for a better look. They were about twenty-five feet away from the stage; a human wall stood between them and the prince.

He was. But Lindsey had only two more pictures left on her roll of film, and she decided not to take any more in case she had a crack at photographing Nessie that day. Still, she didn't want to miss anything, so she stayed where she was on T.J.'s shoulders.

"Scotland has a long proud history," the prince continued amid more applause. "She, like England, has fallen on hard times. But she is strong and hearty. This new highway will bring great strength and joy to Scotland, even as it paves the way for the modern world in this ancient and rugged setting. I commend you men for your hard work. I encourage you to continue, and I pledge to you that every precaution will be taken to ensure your safety. Your country needs you to perform this vital road-building at this important time. I assure you that you will be safe." He paused as the crowd clapped and whistled.

"He isn't saying anything about the monster," Lindsey called down to T.J. in a low voice. He nodded.

"I have brought with me a distinguished professor of biology from the University of Glasgow." The prince stepped aside as the woman came forward with a thin smile. "This is Dr. Margaret Kerr, who has conducted scientific research here at Loch Ness. Some of you have questions about the loch. I have asked her to come with me to answer questions for the press. Thank you all, and God bless you!"

Lindsey frowned. If they were holding a press conference, why were the prince and the professor leaving?

Peter Barrie stepped up to the podium then and motioned for quiet. "Ladies and gentlemen of the press, Dr. Kerr will hold a conference at the Hotel Inverness at twelve o'clock. You must arrange for your own transportation. You may leave after His Royal Highness and Dr. Kerr get into their boat for a tour of the loch. Thank you for coming."

The prince waved at the crowd and turned away. The wind had kicked up, and Lindsey saw His Royal Highness smooth back hair that the breeze had tousled. He, Dr. Kerr, and Peter Barrie then boarded a fancy-looking yacht, while a half-dozen security people followed.

"I have to put you down, Lindsey." T.J. groaned. "My shoulders are starting to hurt."

Lindsey hated to miss anything. She didn't want to take further advantage of T.J., though.

"Wasn't that awesome?" she said as she jumped to the ground.

Andrew nodded and grinned. "I like history this way."

"It was okay," Ben said.

"What's with you anyway?" Sarah chided him. "This is exciting."

"Maybe for you," he said.

Poor Ben! Lindsey hadn't had the opportunity to talk to

him yet about his mother. But she was too excited right now to worry about her moody cousin. That could come later. She wanted to know more about Dr. Kerr and hoped they could go to the press conference. Never mind how they would get near the prince; she just wanted to be as close as possible.

"Can we go to the press conference?" Her eyes moved back and forth between T.J. and Dr. Mac.

"What good would it do, Lindsey?" Mrs. Mac asked. "You won't be able to get in."

"Oh, let's," the minister said. "What else are we doing today that could be more exciting, even if we aren't with the press?" His wife shrugged, then smiled her approval. "We'd better get going, then, if we want to beat this crowd."

They hurried back to the boat but had to wait several minutes for clearance. Then the prince's security people made all boats stay near the shoreline as His Royal Highness's craft cruised around Loch Ness.

"I've heard you mention Dr. Kerr before," Lindsey said to Dr. Mac on their way to Inverness. "Wasn't she your biology professor or something?"

"Yes, and she also acted as my advisor." He paused for a moment. "I had to leave school for a bit while I served in World War I, as so many of my classmates did. Afterward, I majored in theology and lost track of Dr. Kerr. She was a great woman."

"And she knows a lot about Loch Ness?" Sarah asked.

"Yes, indeed. During World War I she conducted research here, looking for the monster. I think I told you she concluded that Loch Ness had been cut off from the North Sea at some point. When that happened, some large aquatic animal—

probably some kind of eel—got caught here."

"Yes, I remember you said something about that. So she would say there's no monster?"

"That's right. Her findings were published in several European scholarly journals." Dr. Mac shook his head. "They didn't generate much attention at the time, though. A war was on. Besides, her research was of a practical, not a sensational, nature."

"Did she have any proof?" T.J. asked.

"That's the truly sad part," Dr. Mac said. "She did take some photos. Unfortunately the conditions were bad, and her equipment was ancient. There wasn't much funding for her project because of the war. All she had to show for her research were dark blots, like modern art." He grinned sheepishly at his wife, who must have loved modern art.

"Now, Guthrie, there's no need to get personal," his wife teased.

"But you believe her?" Lindsey asked.

"I don't have any reason not to."

"So, by bringing her here to reassure the men that there's no monster, the road project will be completed," Lindsey said. "But why not address the road workers as well as the press? Don't they have a right to know what she thinks?"

"Certainly," Dr. Mac said. "But you saw their condition last night. I can imagine that Peter Barrie didn't want to take any chances his men might be rude to the prince."

Lindsey nodded. "That makes sense."

"Besides," Mrs. Mac added, "the men will read her remarks in the papers."

It all seemed so simple, so easily fixed. So why wasn't

Lindsey convinced that the prince's visit would solve the problems surrounding Loch Ness?

Chapter Ten

When they arrived at the stately Hotel Inverness where the press conference would be held, Lindsey saw that security guards had the building surrounded. Quite a throng had gathered to see the prince—and find out more about the monster.

"Only the press is allowed," the bobby repeatedly told spectators as he prevented them from entering the hotel.

"What if we're guests here?" Sarah boldly called out.

T.J. and Lindsey exchanged glances, and T.J. shook his head.

"This is probably the last time she comes with us, Lindsey," Andrew whispered.

She nodded, then added, "Of course I've been striking out a bit myself."

"If you're a guest, go to the back entrance," the guard told Sarah.

Then, to Lindsey's surprise, he waved her toward the entrance.

"Me?" Lindsey pointed to herself.

"The lassie with the camera," he said. "Come, show me your press credentials."

"But I…"

"The girl's all right," a voice interrupted. She turned to see a reporter who had been hanging around the work site.

"Hurry up, then!" The guard waved Lindsey inside. "Go through the double doors, up the stairs, and to the ballroom."

Andrew and Sarah urged her to hurry up, but Lindsey hesitated. "Is it okay, T.J.?"

"I'd say so," he told her. "Make the most of it."

"I will! Thanks!"

Lindsey hurried inside, feeling so pleased she thought she would burst. When she saw the reporter, she thanked him. "That was nice of you."

"Don't mention it," he said, then dashed off.

Lindsey clutched her camera proudly as she followed the guard's directions to the ballroom. Once there, however, she had to wedge herself into the jam-packed hall. And it smelled so strongly of smoke that she started coughing. Why did they have to smoke in that tight space?

Lindsey looked toward the front of the room where she could barely see the stage. Guards stood to each side of it and at floor level in front to keep anyone from getting too close to the prince. A podium with the hotel's seal on the front of it stood on one side of the stage. Heavy cologne smells mixed with the bitter smoke and hung in the air.

Lindsey decided to push closer to the stage so she could take pictures. As she did so, sweating under her heavy tweed skirt and jacket, she remembered that she only had two photos left on her present roll of film. She would have to make the most of them.

She managed to get within a few yards of the stage before determining she could get no closer. She felt almost faint from the press of humans all around her and drew some curious stares from the mostly-male press corps.

The prince and the professor finally arrived, and Lindsey's focus switched from her discomfort to His Royal Highness and Dr. Kerr.

"Thank you for coming here today." Prince Edward smiled brilliantly, seeming calm and unruffled. He had emerged from a windy trip around the loch with not a hair out of place. "I believe you have some questions for me about the Loch Ness phenomenon." He gripped the sides of the podium. Lindsey noticed then, as she snapped a picture, that Peter Barrie and the tourism official were with the prince and Dr. Kerr on the stage. She was almost certain now that the official was the man who had run into the woods after she'd seen Nessie.

"Yes, Your Highness," a Scottish reporter yelled. "Have you seen the monster?"

What a dumb question!

"I have not," the prince replied evenly, "nor do I expect to see such a thing."

"So, you don't believe in it?" another reporter hollered.

"I believe that Dr. Margaret Kerr's theory is correct." He waved toward the professor.

"What theory is that?" another man called out.

"She will share that momentarily," the prince said.

"Is it safe for the road work to continue?" came another question.

"Yes, it is perfectly safe. His Majesty's government is offering a bonus to every road worker for staying on the job and completing it by the original deadline. That is how certain we are that no worker will face danger from this phenomenon."

The crowd murmured, while reporters scribbled furiously in their notebooks.

The prince cleared his throat, and everyone became quiet. "And now, may I introduce Dr. Margaret Kerr of the University of Glasgow? Dr. Kerr has conducted extensive research into the Loch Ness phenomenon. I believe her assessment is accurate and trustworthy. Dr. Kerr."

She curtsied to him, then took her place at the podium. A reporter started yelling something, but she held up her hand to stop him. "I will make a statement, then answer questions."

Lindsey snapped her last picture, making sure to get Prince Edward in the background.

Dr. Kerr came across as if she were giving a university lecture. She told the journalists what Dr. Mac had explained to the Dreamers about the loch getting cut off from the North Sea. She also mentioned how an eel-like animal probably got caught in the lake and then adapted to its new conditions. She gave more details than the minister had provided, and Lindsey was intrigued by the woman's theory. Dr. Kerr explained it in such a way that it made even more sense to Lindsey. Maybe what she had seen was just an eel after all. But why all the fuss? Could an eel have terrified hundreds of people down through the centuries?

"Now that you know what my overall hypothesis is," the professor concluded, "I will be happy to answer any of your questions."

Lindsey was glad for her ease around big words. Otherwise she would have been completely lost.

"So, there's no monster?" someone called out.

"Not so much a monster," Dr. Kerr answered, "as a Loch Ness *animal*."

"Just one?" another reporter asked.

"More likely a class of animal. There cannot have been only one creature sighted for centuries."

"Do you have proof?" one reporter asked rather nastily, Lindsey thought.

Dr. Kerr's face reddened. "If you consider proof to be my years of extensive research, then yes."

"Have you seen these eels?" The man wouldn't let go.

"Yes."

"So, where's the proof? Didn't you take pictures? We have photos now, you know."

Lindsey remembered Dr. Mac saying that while the professor had taken photos, they were of a poor quality. You couldn't tell what the dark blots were. She felt sorry for the woman. If only someone would rush to her defense!

"Just how violent is this animal of yours?" another journalist asked.

"I'm afraid I don't know," Dr. Kerr said, "but I have no reason to believe it would be more aggressive than any other animal."

"Humph!" one reporter grunted loudly. "That's what you get for trusting a woman with something like this!"

The Prince of Wales stepped forward then, and Dr. Kerr immediately began to move back. But the prince took her arm and kept her beside him.

"I have instructed Dr. Kerr to launch a new investigation," he said with great dignity. "When she conducted the last one, her equipment was antiquated. During World War I the government was funding a war and could do little to help her research. But now she will have the best equipment at her disposal. Dr. Kerr will get the so-called proof you demand."

The prince seemed to be getting testy. Then Lindsey noticed something else, something disturbing. David Barbour, the tourism official, kept frowning at the back of Dr. Kerr's head. Then the man caught Lindsey's eye and scowled darkly. What could be eating him?

"Thank you for coming. That is all." Prince Edward and Dr. Kerr stepped into the wings, Mr. Barbour and Peter Barrie following on their heels. The press rushed out like a herd of sheep to file their stories.

Lindsey found T.J. waiting for her near the hotel's entrance. She smiled at the protective look he wore on his face.

"Did you get good pictures?" he asked.

"I think so." She told him about some of the reporters' mean questions. "It's too bad they demanded evidence," she said as they headed outside to their waiting companions.

"I guess so. I do understand, though," T.J. said. "People are really afraid of this thing. We can't expect a few statements to erase centuries of fear."

Lindsey noticed that a light rain had begun to fall, and a crowd, including some journalists, had gathered around Dr. and Mrs. MacRae.

"What's going on?" Lindsey elbowed through the reporters and grabbed Andrew. She was getting good at this.

"Look!" He held out the afternoon edition of the Inverness newspaper. On the front page was a picture of the MacRaes and their croft with its broken window. The caption underneath read: MINISTER'S WINDOW SHATTERED BY UNKNOWN ASSAILANT ON LOCH NESS. ONE OF SEVERAL INCIDENTS ON PROPERTY.

Lindsey struggled to read the accompanying story as people

jostled her. After a few minutes, she finally gave up. Dr. and Mrs. Mac were trying really hard to escape the crowd. The guard who had admitted Lindsey to the press conference finally told the reporters to leave.

"I can't understand how this got into the paper," Mrs. Mac said, crying. Her husband helped her down the steep marble stairs of the hotel so she didn't slip in her high heels.

"Neither can I," he said, frowning. "You folks didn't tell anyone, did you?"

"No," they all said at once.

"Of course you didn't. It's just that from every possible angle, this is so strange."

"We'd better get home to Burnsey," Mrs. Mac said. "I hope he's all right by himself."

Lindsey wanted to reassure the woman, but she was worried, too. She quickly told everyone about the press conference with Dr. Kerr, concluding with the part about the reporters demanding proof. "The Prince of Wales said she's going to undertake a new investigation."

"She has her work cut out for her," Mrs. Mac grumbled. "These reporters are like jackals."

"You know, dear," her husband began, "I'm concerned about Burnsey, too, but it's way past lunch time, and we haven't eaten yet. I've had this hankering for a steak and kidney pie. It started last night around two of the clock, and I just couldn't get it off my mind. I thought about that time…" And the pastor was off on another tangent.

"I didn't pack a picnic lunch for us, Guthrie," Mrs. Mac interrupted him gently. "Oh, I do wish I had. Then we could eat on the way home."

"Are you folks hungry?" the minister asked the rest of them.

They all said they were, very hungry.

"I could eat a horse," Andrew said.

"Let's slip into that café." The minister pointed across the street. "It's usually pretty quiet there. It's also dark inside, so no one should bother us." He grinned impishly. "I don't think they have horse on the menu, though, Andrew. And Mary," he turned to his wife, "try not to worry about Burnsey. He can take care of himself."

They all ate a relaxing lunch, in spite of the waiter's remark about seeing Lindsey in the morning newspaper. Lindsey enjoyed her meal of roast beef and oat cakes, which was what T.J. also ordered. The boys tried lamb stew, and Sarah had something called cock-a-leaky soup. Dr. Mac ordered his steak and kidney pie, and Mrs. Mac had herring. Although the food was delicious, Lindsey was sure her brother was lost without his ketchup.

After hot tea and a layered dessert called trifle—pieces of cake and fruit drenched in syrup and pudding—the group waddled toward the door, where Dr. Mac bumped into his former professor, Margaret Kerr.

"Dr. Kerr!" he exclaimed.

"Can it possibly be Guthrie MacRae?" Dr. Kerr was clearly delighted to see him again.

They shook hands warmly.

"This is my wife, Mary, whom you've met before. And these are our friends, T.J., Lindsey, Andrew, Ben, and Sarah Wakesnoris."

Everyone shook hands and smiled at the professor.

"Were you dining here?" Dr. Mac asked. "We didn't see you."

"Yes. The staff put me in a private room with the Prince of Wales." She lowered her voice. "Neither of us wanted any more attention. Besides, we had some business to conduct."

"Is he still here?" Sarah asked breathlessly.

"No. They let him out the back door."

"Too bad!" Sarah snapped her fingers in disappointment.

"T.J. and his family are visiting us from the United States," Dr. Mac said. "Lindsey had the good fortune of being admitted to your press conference because she was wearing such a nice camera. She told us that you'll be doing a new investigation of the Loch Ness—"

"Please don't say 'monster,'" she groaned.

"I won't then." Everyone laughed, even Ben. Margaret Kerr was a delightful person.

"Yes." She sighed a bit heavily. "I am completely unprepared for this. The prince came up with the idea on the spot during the news conference. Anyway, Guthrie, how is the ministry these days?"

"Fine," he said. "I am as excited about serving the Lord now as I was when I first answered his call."

"I see. Then you feel you've chosen the right profession?" Her tone was slightly tense.

When someone scooted around them and opened the door, Lindsey saw that the rain had stopped. But it was still chilly, and she shivered.

"Yes indeed," Dr. Mac said.

"Well, I'm glad for you. However, I've always been sorry that you gave up fact for fiction."

Lindsey gaped at her. She couldn't believe the professor had been so blunt. How would Dr. Mac respond?

He smiled graciously. "It would seem that we are both going down the same paths as before. I am still a poet, and you haven't yet discovered the language of the soul."

The professor looked surprised, then smiled slightly. "Touché! I deserved that. Well, now that we're through getting in our jabs, what's everyone doing next?"

"We're heading home," Mrs. Mac said. "Where are you staying, Dr. Kerr?"

She suddenly laughed. "I have no idea! I wasn't planning to stop here or do this investigation. According to His Royal Highness, though, I'll be here for as long as it takes to get some pictures of the loch animals." She shook her head. "Good thing I'm the department chairman at the university. Otherwise I might be fired for this! Goodness! I have no clothes and no assistant. I'll have to wire for everything to be sent. The students are on holiday, though." She looked befuddled.

"Dr. Kerr, we have only a small, crowded croft on the loch to offer you, but you and I are about the same size," Mrs. Mac said. "We'd be delighted to have you stay with us."

"Indeed we would!" the minister said heartily. "If you would so honor me, I'd love to act as your research assistant. I haven't forgotten all that you taught me. There's more in my head than theology and literature, and I'm still as fascinated as ever with the Loch Ness animal."

The professor seemed a little knocked off balance by their offer. "Well, if you don't mind. It would be great to stay right on the loch. Why, I'd love to!"

Lindsey was pleased to see there were no hard feelings between the minister and his former professor. It would certainly be interesting to share a room with Sarah and Dr. Kerr!

Chapter Eleven

On the way back to the croft, Lindsey noticed a good deal of activity on and near the loch. Some men were out in their boats searching for the beastie. They called out to Dr. Mac and the rest of them, asking if they had seen anything. And ended up disappointed. Lindsey pointed out a row of ugly silver trailers lined up on the road across from the castle.

"That's the press caravan," T.J. explained. "I heard some reporters talking about that earlier today."

Just then two men on the shore begged them to get off the loch. "You'll be swallowed like Jonah!"

"What or who is Jonah?" Sarah asked Lindsey.

This wouldn't be easy since Sarah had barely a nodding acquaintance with the Scriptures. "It's a Bible story," Lindsey said simply, then noticed that Dr. Kerr was listening, too. Lindsey figured she didn't believe in God either, not after criticizing Dr. Mac for going into the ministry.

"About what?"

"Jonah was a prophet who ran away from God."

"Yes, and a whale swallowed Jonah," Andrew said.

"How awful!" Sarah scrunched her face in disgust.

"Yeah, but the whale spit him out after a while," Ben said.

"You don't mean that?" she asked skeptically.

"Sure," he said. "It's in the Bible."

"Another one!" Sarah sniffed.

"Another what?" Ben frowned.

"Tall tale, that's what. I can't believe you people believe those fairy stories."

Lindsey quickly prayed about how to respond. She longed for her friend to believe in the God of the Bible. And maybe she could even influence Dr. Kerr. As if in answer to her prayer, she suddenly remembered reading about a man who, some-time in the 1800s, was swallowed by a large fish and lived to tell about it.

"Is that true, Dr. Kerr?" Sarah asked the professor after Lindsey finished her story.

She sniffed and ran a hand through her blowing hair. "I'm afraid so."

This quieted Sarah. "Well, I still don't believe in God or the Bible, so let's drop it."

There seemed nothing more for Lindsey to say—at least for the time being.

They arrived at the croft close to four o'clock. The Loch's boat traffic had slowed their progress considerably, and the journey from Inverness had taken twice as long as usual. Just as they docked, Lindsey spotted a man running away from the house into a nearby stand of trees. The Haunted Highlander! There could be no doubt about it. She wondered if anyone else had seen him. Everyone but Mrs. Mac was concentrating on land-ing the boat.

When they had docked and tied the boat securely to its moorings, Mrs. Mac raced up the hill as fast as her high heels would allow. Lindsey was right behind her, curious to know if

Burnsey was all right. She wondered what the Highlander was up to, if he had hurt the dog or the croft in any way. He could be the one causing mischief for the MacRaes.

To everyone's relief, Burnsey was just fine. When Mrs. Mac unlocked the door, the little Westie jumped all over his mistress with the abandon of a kite in a high wind. Burnsey took turns greeting everyone—except Dr. Kerr. He approached her almost respectfully.

"Well, see this!" Dr. Mac exclaimed. "Looks like you're the guest of honor."

"No, it's just that I don't care much for dogs," she said.

Dr. Kerr was outspoken, but there was something about her that Lindsey liked. Although she was every inch a professional woman, the way she wore her hair and her clothes told Lindsey she had a soft side to her as well.

Mrs. Mac ushered the professor inside and started organizing some outfits for her to wear, while the boys busied themselves carrying a cot into Lindsey and Sarah's room. The girls made it up with sheets and blankets, and Mrs. Mac found an extra pillow.

"You can have my bed if you like it better," Lindsey offered when Dr. Kerr entered their room, bearing several outfits.

"No, thank you, dear. I won't be displacing anyone more than I've already done. Besides, this cot looks just fine." Dr. Kerr promptly lay down on it to take a nap.

In the evening they all enjoyed a light supper of soup and oat cakes, then talked until ten o'clock about the Loch Ness Monster. Lindsey loved listening to the stories from Dr. Kerr's first investigation. One especially fascinated her.

"On one particular day," the scientist began, "I was observing the loch when a breeze created some ripples on the surface.

Until then it had been flat and calm. Some minutes later, I saw an object like a head with a long, thin neck."

Lindsey was so engrossed in the story that she accidentally stuck her elbow in a jam-covered oat cake. Everyone laughed as she tried to clean the glop off her sweater.

"I got my camera ready," the professor continued, "but the object disappeared."

"Did it return?" asked Lindsey.

The elegant woman nodded. "Yes. Not more than a few moments later, I saw it again. I started taking pictures. My excitement grew and grew," she said, her voice rising, "as the creature appeared, then submerged several times."

Everyone listened intently.

"I felt the excitement surge within me as a body appeared." Dr. Kerr's voice suddenly dropped dramatically. "The so-called beastie took off with a great rustle of its wings and soared sky-ward."

"It was a bird!" Lindsey cried.

Dr. Kerr nodded solemnly. "It was a bird," she said with a twinkle in her eye.

"What a bummer!"

"But you did get to see the monster sometime while you were exploring," Andrew said.

"Animal." Dr. Kerr was determined about its name. "Yes, I did, uh…"

"Andrew."

"Yes, Andrew. But I'm afraid the pictures weren't believable."

"So now you'll get some good ones," Lindsey said. "The Prince of Wales will get the right supplies and equipment, and you'll prove your theory about Loch Ness."

Lindsey was so excited that she accidentally kicked Burnsey who was resting near her on the floor. She quickly apologized to the dog, but he didn't seem impressed.

"That's the general idea," said the professor a little doubtfully.

"Are eels deadly?" Lindsey asked.

"Why do you ask?" The professor raised her eyebrows.

"It's just that if they weren't, why would people be that afraid of a so-called monster?"

Dr. Kerr pursed her lips, then said, "The Loch Ness animal could easily ram a boat hard enough to give it a good jolt."

"Would it attack a person?" Ben asked.

"Maybe. If it were provoked. I doubt," Dr. Kerr said, "that it would deliberately attack."

"Did the mons—uh, eels scare you?" Andrew asked.

Dr. Kerr shifted. "Why all the questions?"

"I believe you about the eels," Lindsay said quickly, "but I think they must be pretty scary. Not everyone makes up fantastic stories about Nessie."

"I see."

"By the way, are you a zooist?" Andrew asked.

Lindsey burst out laughing as her brother's face grew red with embarrassment. "That's zoologist," she corrected him.

Andrew's goof-up didn't seem to bother Dr. Kerr. "My official title is paleontologist, but like a zoologist, I study the animal kingdom. My field is simply a little broader."

"What's a paleontologist?" Ben asked, pronouncing the word carefully.

"They're into geological periods and fossils and stuff, right, Dr. Kerr?" Lindsey said before the professor could explain.

"Right."

"Well, it's late, and we all need our sleep." Mrs. Mac got up and delicately stretched her long legs and arms. "Tomorrow is bound to be a big day."

The professor frowned. "I can't imagine how His Majesty is going to organize everything."

By now Lindsey felt a little guilty for laughing at her brother. She walked over to him on her way to the bedroom.

"Hey, Andrew, I'm sorry about that."

He shrugged. "It's okay."

"I thought I was getting better about not teasing you."

He regarded his sister warmly. "Don't worry. You are."

The following morning a messenger at the door intruded upon their breakfast. Lindsey was grateful for the break, though. Mrs. Mac had just piled her plate high with herring.

"Eat up, lassie, you're as thin as a thistle!" the woman had said.

"Oh, for Wheaties and overripe bananas," Lindsey muttered to her brother. She started the now-familiar routine of feeding the dog under the table. It wasn't working as well as at first, though. Apparently Sarah, Andrew, and Ben all had the same idea, and Burnsey looked as if he were about to explode with herring.

"Yes, she's here," Lindsey heard Mrs. Mac say to the person at the door. "Professor Kerr, it's someone for you."

Dr. Kerr laid her linen napkin on the table and excused herself. Her eagerness reminded Lindsey of a child's at a birthday party. And for good reason. When the scientist returned several moments later, she held up a set of keys.

"The prince has made good on his promise. A boat with equipment is waiting for us in Inverness."

"Let's get hopping then!" Lindsey cried.

"Lindsey!" T.J. gave her a warning look.

"Did I say something wrong?" she asked, wide-eyed.

"We are in the middle of breakfast," he reminded her.

"Oh."

Dr. Kerr laughed. "She's expressing my feelings precisely." She turned to her hostess. "Would you mind awfully, Mrs. MacRae, if we went just now?"

"Not at all," she said cheerfully. "Why don't you just go ahead, and I'll clean everything up?"

"That's hardly fair, dear," Dr. Mac said. "We can get this later."

"And leave Burnsey to devour the entire contents of the table?" She laughed. "Remember that time we turned our backs on him, and he ate an entire plate of sausages?"

"Yes, I remember." Dr. Mac chuckled. "But don't worry, Mary. We'll take Burnsey with us."

"No, no. You just go ahead. I'm a little tired today anyway. I'd rather stay behind."

Everyone—except Ben—was ready to go within minutes.

"Aren't you coming?" Lindsey asked him.

"I'll help Mrs. Mac."

"She'll probably want you to come along."

"We've already discussed it. Lindsey, I don't want to be on this trip. Just leave me alone, please."

Something stabbed at her feelings. "I was just—"

"It's okay," he quickly said. "I know you're trying to be

nice, but I just need to be alone."

Lindsey left, knowing that they would soon need to have that talk.

The Prince of Wales had outdone himself. The boat he'd sent for Dr. Kerr was as seaworthy as any of His Majesty's royal vessels. New and sparkling, it carried the insignia of the Royal Navy. It had all the latest photographic equipment, telescopes, navigational gear, and even a bathroom in which the soap and towels bore the prince's personal seal. It was sparkling clean and sleek and classy, and dwarfed the minister's boat by several yards.

"There's just one problem," Dr. Kerr said after they had inspected the enormous yacht.

"Which is?" Lindsey asked.

Dr. Kerr frowned. "There's no crew."

"I guess we're it." Dr. Mac clapped his hands. "Believe me, I'll be good to this lassie." He ran his hands over the heavily polished steering wheel. "This is a dream come true for me."

The professor laughed. "Good! Let's make mine come true as well."

"What does she mean?" Sarah whispered to Lindsey.

"I think she wants to get proof for her theory about the Loch Ness Mons—uh, animal."

"And the sooner the better," T.J. said behind them. "Did you girls see this latest headline?"

He showed them the daily Glasgow paper he had picked up while Dr. Kerr was getting her boat. The headline read: NESSIE RIDES AGAIN. Below the headline was a picture of an animal with a lengthy neck and a small head as it skimmed Loch Ness's surface. The caption said the photo was taken by an "observer."

They showed the photo to Dr. Kerr. Her hair blew softly in the breeze as she shook her head.

"Don't you believe it?" Lindsey asked.

"No, I do not."

"But it's a real picture," Sarah argued, as she thumped the paper. "Someone actually saw this."

"Seeing may be believing," Dr. Kerr said, "but sometimes it isn't everything."

Sarah frowned and then gave Lindsey a puzzled look.

"Look at this headline." Andrew held up another paper. T.J. and the girls leaned closer to see it. SCIENTIST CONFIRMS MONSTER.

Dr. Kerr sighed deeply and rolled her eyes while Andrew read a paragraph that completely twisted the professor's words.

"They refuse to believe there's no monster," she said when he had finished reading. "The truth is it's simply a species of animal that doesn't like being around people much."

"We'll show them!" Sarah said spiritedly.

Dr. Kerr put an arm around her shoulders. "Thank God for people like you."

"I thought you didn't believe in God," Dr. Mac teased.

His former professor blushed as the others laughed.

They spent most of the day getting used to the new boat and testing their new gear. Lindsey especially loved playing with one of four cameras the prince had loaned Dr. Kerr. This also gave her an excuse to keep a lookout for Nessie as they cruised up and down the lake.

On their way to the road site at around three-thirty, Dr. Kerr came to stand beside Lindsey. "You haven't seen our friend, have you?" she asked.

"No," Lindsey said.

"I don't think you will today."

"Why not?"

"Too much boat traffic. And I don't believe we'll see them anywhere near Urquhart Castle. Plus the road workers have blasted how many times today?"

"Two."

"The animals I saw twenty years ago are very shy."

"What should we do?" Lindsey asked.

"I think a night excursion farther down the loch would be helpful."

"If you don't mind, Dr. Kerr, I'd like to stop by the press area near the road work before we head back. Do you think we could do that? Maybe we can learn something new."

"That would be fine," she said briskly. "I think we've accomplished a lot for one day."

They got to the press caravans nearly an hour later, and Lindsey had an idea.

"I have a lot of film to develop," she told her companions. "Would it be okay if I tried to find someone who could help me?" She nodded toward the press headquarters. "There's probably a darkroom there."

"I don't mind," Dr. Mac said. "I think I'll just stay on the boat, though. I'm having great fun with my new toy." His eyes twinkled.

"It is wonderful," Andrew said.

"Stay with me, then, son." The minister's invitation was warm-hearted. "We can go over this ship together."

Sarah stretched and yawned. "I'll stay, too, then. All this wind and motion are making me tired."

"I'll check some of this equipment while you're away," Dr. Kerr said. "I'm still not too sure about the telescope."

"That's fine with me," Lindsey said. "I'll only be a half hour or so."

"Not so fast, Lindsey," T.J. told her. "I'll go with you."

"That's all right. I can go by myself to find a darkroom."

The teacher's brows rose slightly. "No, Lindsey," he said slowly. "Reporters can be a rough bunch."

"I'll be okay."

"I'll make sure you are."

As they walked toward the press trailers, or caravans as the Scottish called them, Lindsey noticed that there weren't too many reporters around. They did find one, though, and T.J. asked if there was a darkroom.

"Over there." The reporter nodded toward the one farthest away.

"May I use it?" Lindsey asked.

"Makes no matter to me."

"Where is everyone?"

"Out on the loch. Everybody wants the next exclusive photo."

Within moments they stood at the door of the tiny structure. Lindsey reached out to turn the doorknob, but a voice inside stopped her.

"We seem to be doing a good job of fooling all of the people all of the time!" a deep voice said.

Chapter Twelve

Lindsey and T.J. froze like statues as the Scottish-accented voices continued.

"I didn't think that dummy monster was very good at all," said a second man.

"Yeah, well, good help is hard to find these days," came the response.

"No matter. Your carpenter friend did a good enough job to get those photos in the papers. Don't worry about it."

Lindsey leaned closer to T.J. "I think it's that Will Campbell guy," she whispered.

"Shhh!" T.J. hissed, lifting a finger to his lips.

Lindsey nodded, then turned to listen once more.

"So, what's the next step?" asked the man whom Lindsey thought was the reporter.

"I don't think that girl has figured out who I am. Right now the major fly in the ointment is this she-professor."

"I know what you mean."

"If she really does get the pictures she claims that she can, we're out of business."

His companion gave a dull laugh. "No tourist money, eh?"

"Yeah, but Nessie's also a tradition. It would be like finding out there's no Santa Claus."

"So, what do we do?"

Both Lindsey and T.J. crouched closer to the door.

Lindsey's heart pounded, and her ears rang as she listened tensely.

"Stop her."

There was a brief pause. "Well, we already stopped one of them!" The other man laughed harshly.

"So let's get to work!"

T.J. grabbed Lindsey by the arm as the men began to move around inside. They had just enough time to hide behind a large bush before the men slunk out the door of the trailer. Unfortunately, Lindsey couldn't see their faces. She did see, however, that while the men were of average height, one of them was noticeably heavier.

"T.J., what are we going to do?" Lindsey asked tensely after the men were gone.

He got up and helped her to her feet. They brushed off dust and pieces of leaves from their clothes. "I'll have to give that some thought."

She tugged on his sleeve. "Let's go warn the others."

"Not just yet." He stood firm and regarded her sternly. "I'll decide when that time comes."

"All right," she said slowly, as if doing him a big favor. "I wonder what they meant about already stopping someone."

T.J.'s jaw tightened. "I don't know."

"What should we do now?"

"Let's not see about those photos just yet."

"Maybe we can talk to some road workers before we go back to the boat," Lindsey suggested. "They might have more information than we have now."

T.J. looked doubtful but agreed to go with her. As they walked to the worker's area, Lindsey's head was spinning. "So

Dr. Kerr's right. There really is no Loch Ness Monster, is there, T.J.? What I saw was probably part of this hoax."

"No, Lindsey, I don't think there is a monster. Just some very misunderstood marine creature or creatures who live around here."

She sighed and shoved her hands into her jacket pockets. "I'm disappointed."

T.J. pursed his lips. "Yes, I guess you must be. But keep in mind, Lindsey, that whatever is out there is still worth knowing about."

"I guess you're right. And we're going to get to the bottom of it, aren't we?"

"I'd say so, based on my other adventures in time travel."

"I hope we can help Dr. Kerr get her pictures," Lindsey said. "If she does photograph Nessie, the whole world will know the truth, including that those guys are faking monster pictures for the newspapers. I'll bet that guy I saw right after I spotted Nessie was one of the men we just heard!" Lindsey was so excited she forgot to take a breath. "We could take a picture back with us—a real one, I mean—and everyone for all time would know the truth about Nessie."

"Slow down!" T.J. laughed, then sobered. "One step at a time, Lindsey. God has a purpose for our being here. Let's not run ahead of him."

They only talked to the road workers for a few minutes. The men were simply too busy to chat. Lindsey noticed there were more of them around, however, since the prince had given his speech. She guessed that his offer of bonus money for completing the road on time had motivated the workers.

Back on the boat, Lindsey found everyone in such high

spirits that she didn't say anything about the conversation she and T.J. had overheard. The trip to the croft was uneventful, other than the dozen or so monster hunters on the loch searching for Nessie, and slowing their progress. Dr. Mac had to swerve out of another vessel's way at least twice. "They're so intent on finding the monster, they're not paying attention to what they're doing," he grumbled after the second time.

When the croft came into view, Lindsey felt a chill run down her spine. "Look!" she cried.

Ben was stumbling down the bank to the boat launch, waving his arms and yelling. Burnsey was on the boy's heels yipping and jumping. Lindsey strained to hear what Ben was saying, but the boat's motor drowned him out. Lindsey couldn't wait for Dr. Mac to properly moor the boat. She vaulted over the side and ran up to her cousin.

"What's wrong?" she asked fearfully.

"Mrs. Mac is missing," he cried breathlessly.

"Missing! What do you mean?"

"Oh, Lindsey, I feel just terrible."

By then Dr. Mac had left the boat in T.J.'s hands and had joined Lindsey and Ben. When Ben told him the news, Dr. Mac's face went white, like a bleached sheet. "What do you mean, she's missing?" he asked shakily. "What happened, son?"

The others had caught up and began to press Ben for details.

"Mrs. Mac went out to hang up wash," Lindsey's cousin began. "I was playing some records and reading a book, but then I suddenly realized she wasn't anywhere around. I thought maybe she came back inside and I just hadn't heard her. Then Burnsey started barking really loud. He was outside at the time. But when I went out, I couldn't find Mrs. Mac." Ben was trembling now.

"Did you see anyone around the croft?" Dr. Mac asked.

"No, sir, I didn't."

"What time did this happen?" The minister's voice and hands shook, and he seemed to be struggling for control.

"About an hour ago. Oh, Dr. Mac, I'm so sorry!" Ben cried.

"Sorry?" Dr. Mac looked surprised.

"I should've taken better care of her."

"Now, don't you worry, son." He took Ben by the shoulders. "My wife takes good care of herself. It isn't your fault." As soothing as he tried to be, though, the minister was noticeably upset.

Just then a commotion rose at the dock. Two police officers and a handful of reporters sped toward them on a boat.

"What in the world!" Dr. Mac exclaimed.

"How can they know about this already?" Sarah asked.

Ben threw up his hands. "I didn't tell anyone."

The police questioned them inside the croft for over two hours. During that time, Lindsey and T.J. told them about the conversation they had overheard at the darkroom trailer.

"Do you think the two incidents could be related?" T.J. asked.

The younger policeman nodded carefully. "It's quite possible. You say you didn't get a good look at the men?"

"No." Lindsey shook her head. "We only saw their backs. They were of average height, and one was on the heavy side."

"That's how I remember them, too," T.J. said.

"I think I recognized one of their voices," Lindsey continued. "He sounded like a reporter I've met here, a guy named Will Campbell."

The police stared at each other. "He's a darn good reporter," the older one said.

"He may be, but I think he's involved in some kind of scheme," Lindsey said. She told them about seeing Barbour right after spotting Nessie and overhearing Barbour and Campbell talking in the restaurant.

The older officer wrote something down in a tattered notebook. "Isn't there some oddball Highlander who lives around these parts?"

"Yes," Dr. Mac said. "Some people say he's a spirit, but I think he's simply a recluse."

"Have you ever spoken to him?"

"No. I've tried, but he isn't very social."

"Guthrie, do you think he may have kidnapped your wife?" Dr. Kerr asked.

"I doubt it. Of course, we need to exhaust every possibility, but I don't think the Highlander means anyone harm. He just doesn't seem to like being around people."

After a few more questions, the policemen led Dr. Mac on a search for his wife. Lindsey wanted to go with them but was not permitted. Instead, she stayed behind while a growing number of reporters jostled on the lawn, taking pictures of the croft and waiting for interviews.

T.J. led a prayer for Mrs. Mac's safety, one that even the professor and Sarah participated in. Afterward Sarah told Lindsey, "Right now I'm really hoping there is a God. Mrs. Mac is a really nice person."

Lindsey hugged her friend. "There is, Sarah. I promise, there is."

It was nightfall when Dr. Mac and the police returned.

Lindsey jumped off her chair and raced over to the men for news, only to hear there had been no sign of the pastor's wife.

"I'm going into Inverness with the police," Dr. Mac told them. "We need to widen the investigation beyond the croft and its vicinity."

"Do you want one of us to go with you?" T.J. asked.

"Thanks, but no. I'll be fine. Do let's have a prayer together, though."

He gathered everyone around, including the police, and prayed in a broken voice for his wife's safety. Then he left. And Lindsey forgot about the Loch Ness Monster, at least for the time being.

Around seven o'clock Sarah mentioned that they hadn't eaten supper yet.

"You're right, and we need to keep up our strength," Dr. Kerr said. "C'mon, Sarah. Let's you and I get some soup going."

As they went to work in the kitchen, T.J. and Andrew slept sitting up on the couch, while Ben joined Lindsey on the floor by the fire.

"Are you okay?" she asked.

"I guess. I feel real bad about Mrs. Mac, though. Do you think she's all right?"

"Let's hope for the best."

They were both quiet for a moment, then Ben said, "I'm sorry I've been in such a bad mood."

Lindsey didn't need to ask what he meant. His mood had been pretty obvious. "Do you want to talk about it?"

"I'd like to, that is, if you don't mind."

"I don't mind. I'd like to help if I can."

"It's just that everyone's pushing…" Ben's voice rose, then

more softly he said, "Everyone's pushing my mom to get a new husband. They act like it's as simple as buying a new sweater or something. I get really mad." He balled his chubby hands into fists.

"You don't want a new dad, do you?"

"Why would I want a new dad when I've had the best there is?" He tugged at a piece of newspaper from a stack near the fireplace and started worrying it with his thick fingers.

"No one could replace Uncle Mark." Lindsey put her hand on Ben's arm. "I miss him, too."

"You do?"

"Sure. I think about him a lot."

They listened to a piece of wood hiss loudly, then pop. In the background they could hear Sarah and Dr. Kerr running water and clinking pots and pans.

"I was boiling mad when I saw Mom and T.J. having a good time," Ben went on. "And right before that, Sarah said her dad and my mom should get together." He tossed the piece of crumbled newspaper into the fire. It burned up within seconds.

"I guess that would upset me, too," Lindsey said. "I mean, if I were you, which I'm not. But I can understand how you would feel that way." She sighed. "I'm talking too much again."

"I don't mind."

"Ben, I have something to tell you."

He looked at her curiously.

"I don't think you need to worry about your mom remarrying right now."

"Why not?"

"Well, once I asked her—I think it was a couple months

ago when we were watching a movie about a widow—if she ever wanted to get married again."

"You did? What did she say?" Ben asked eagerly.

"She said maybe someday." Ben's face fell. "But not for a really long time." Lindsey got that part in quickly. "She said the most important thing to her right now is being a good mother."

"She did?"

"Uh-huh. She said that after you've grown up she might be open to a new husband, if that's God's will. But for now, you're her first concern."

The look of relief on Ben's face brought tears to Lindsey's eyes. Later, as she went to the supper table, she was grateful that at least one major problem had been solved. Now if they could just find Mrs. Mac, and if they could just photograph Nessie and expose the hoax.

Chapter Thirteen

The following morning Lindsey awakened before anyone else and tiptoed to the kitchen for a glass of water. Burnsey sidled over to her from his spot near the fireplace, and she cuddled him. Lindsey didn't know if Dr. Mac had stayed in Inverness or if he had come home late.

As she stood at the kitchen sink looking out the window, the mysterious Highlander suddenly appeared right in front of her. She stood stock still, shocked right down to her toes. But the man wore a pleading expression, so Lindsey recovered her wits and quickly moved toward the back door to see what he wanted. Unfortunately, a member of the press spotted him, and the Highlander raced off with two reporters in hot pursuit.

Now several reporters advanced toward the door to talk to Lindsey. She lifted her hand to stop them. "Please be quiet!" she said in a loud whisper. "Everyone's still sleeping."

They backed off slightly, then one of them held out a copy of his newspaper. "Would you like the morning paper?"

A fresh breeze from the loch whipped through Lindsey's hair as she accepted it through the back door. "Is Will Campbell out there with you?" she asked on a sudden impulse. He wasn't. "Well, please let me know if he comes."

"Could you give us an interview?" one of them asked.

"I don't think so."

"But this is big news. You could give us an exclusive!"

Lindsey stiffened. "These people are my friends. I'm more interested in them than a scoop."

She closed the door, then went to Mrs. Mac's favorite chair in the living room and examined the front page. "Oh, brother!" she moaned. HAUNTED HIGHLANDER KIDNAPS MINISTER'S WIFE, she read aloud. The article described how Mrs. Mac had disappeared. It spoke about a weird connection between the Haunted Highlander and the Loch Ness Monster that stretched back for centuries. The article concluded by saying that the MacRaes might be paying a price for taking in Dr. Kerr because she didn't believe in Nessie. "This is so bogus," Lindsey said, tossing the paper aside. Their trouble had begun long before Dr. Kerr came into the picture.

"What's bogus?" Dr. Mac appeared before Lindsey, giving her a terrible start. His face was lined with worry, and he didn't look like he'd slept at all.

"Dr. Mac!" she exclaimed. "I didn't know you were here." She paused. "It's this headline."

Dr. Mac sniffed his disapproval as he glanced at the paper she showed him. Then he dropped it on the couch and sank down next to it. Burnsey hopped up next to him, burying his furry head in the pastor's lap.

"Was there any progress last night?" Lindsey asked.

He shook his head.

"Dr. Mac, I think this could be related to those men T.J. and I heard at the press trailer."

"It makes more sense than any other theory I've heard." He grunted. "Haunted Highlander indeed!"

Lindsey then told him about seeing the strange man just a few minutes earlier. "It was like he was trying to tell me something," she said.

"Maybe he was," Dr. Mac said hopefully. "Let's go look for him. I know where he lives."

"That's a great idea! Should we go now?"

"Yes."

Lindsey quickly dressed, then she and Dr. Mac slipped quietly out the back door to go in search of the Highlander. He was not in his croft, however, nor was he anywhere else they looked on the moor.

"I'll bet those reporters spooked him," Lindsey said.

"I'm afraid you're right."

On the way back to the croft Lindsey repeated her story of the events at the press trailer. "You know, Dr. Mac," she concluded, "I don't think the police are going to question Will Campbell. I think they like him."

Dr. Mac ran a hand over his unshaved face. "They do at that, Lindsey. He was right there last night at the station, questioning the top detectives about this case. It seems he's one of their cronies."

"Then we have to do something ourselves."

"You really are a remarkable young lady!" he said. "What, pray tell, are you thinking?"

"Dr. Kerr says Nessie will be easier to track at night. She says it's quieter then, and most boats around this area aren't equipped for night use."

"Aye," he answered in Scottish fashion.

"I think we should go out on the loch tonight to look, not just for Nessie, but for Mrs. Mac, too."

They walked quietly for a few moments. "You realize we'll probably be followed?" he said finally. "I mean, all those reporters camped by my house!"

"That's the idea." Her eyes sparkled.

Dr. Mac stared at her. "I see."

"I'm hoping to make us a target for Will Campbell and his partner. They might lead us to her. And Dr. Kerr may see Nessie and get the photos that will show the world what the monster really is."

"You realize this may be dangerous."

Lindsey nodded. "I know. We'll just have to pray extra hard, won't we, Dr. Mac?"

At breakfast that morning Dr. Kerr offered to leave. The minister, however, wouldn't hear of it.

"But I seem to be bringing you such bad luck—"

"I don't believe in luck, Dr. Kerr. I believe in God."

"But if there is a God, why has this happened to Mary? She's such a good person."

"There is a God," the pastor said quietly yet firmly. "And he's with Mary as surely now as he's ever been. How can I accept good from him and not trust him when the enemy of our souls strikes?" His voice cracked.

"I wish I believed like that," Dr. Kerr said after a moment.

"You can."

Lindsey glanced at Sarah. Her friend's eyes were all shiny, as if this was affecting her powerfully. Maybe God was finally getting through.

"Give me time, Guthrie."

"I can, but you never know how much time you have," he said.

Did Dr. Mac believe his wife might not be alive? It was too awful to think about.

"Dr. Kerr," Lindsey said boldly, changing the subject, "let me tell you about a plan we have."

By nightfall most of the reporters had given up trying to interview Dr. Mac and gone home. As Dr. Kerr busily prepared for their Nessie search, Ben helped Lindsey get dinner together. It wasn't much—leftover soup and biscuits—but no one seemed to be thinking about food. Lindsey's spirits were high as she anticipated what the evening might bring. The plan was to go out on the loch around eleven o'clock in the prince's well-equipped boat.

The police called just after nine to say they didn't yet have any news about Mrs. Mac. As the minister spoke to them, Lindsey had a brainstorm. She tugged his arm to get his attention.

"What?" he asked, cupping his hand over the receiver.

"Tell them we're going out with Dr. Kerr," she whispered. "If Will Campbell's at the station with them, he'll probably hear about it and follow us."

Dr. Mac stared at her briefly, then nodded. "No, I'm still here," he told the policeman on the other end. "Well, thank you. By the way, I'm going out with Dr. Kerr tonight to look for Nessie." Lindsey groaned inwardly at his clumsy wording. "Yes, that's right. We will." Then he hung up. "I think everything's set," he said.

"Not quite." Sarah gave a sheepish grin.

Dr. Mac looked puzzled. "What do you mean?" he asked.

"You haven't prayed about our trip."

He clapped a hand to his forehead. "Thank you, Sarah."

At 11:15 a thin mist swirled around the croft, as T.J., Dr. Kerr, Sarah, and the boys traipsed down to the prince's boat. Then they returned, lugging equipment that was too valuable to keep on board, things like cameras and portable navigation devices. To their relief, all the reporters were gone.

Lindsey and Dr. Mac were the last ones out of the croft. As Dr. Mac locked the door, Burnsey at his side, a large figure emerged from the fog. Lindsey yelped.

"What in the—" Dr. Mac gasped as he saw the Haunted Highlander, and Burnsey started barking.

"What is it?" T.J. called from the boat.

Lindsey recovered first and stared at the Highlander. "What d-do you want?"

Unruly white hair crowned the Highlander's massive head. His pink cheeks seemed out of place on his bulky body.

"I have something to tell you," he said.

"What?" Dr. Mac sounded irritated, but Lindsey thought he was probably just scared.

"I didn't take your wife. Some other men did."

T.J. yelled again, then they heard him bounding toward the croft, the others on his heels. The Highlander took a few steps back as they approached him with startled expressions.

"They won't hurt you," Lindsey said softly. For some reason, she was no longer afraid of him.

"I'm not used to people," he mumbled.

"You seem familiar," Dr. Kerr said. "Do we know each other?"

"You might say that." He bowed slightly. "I used to teach at Glasgow University. Years ago."

"My goodness!" she exclaimed. "Gillespie's your name, isn't it?"

He nodded. "I don't care to be around people, so I came here. To my roots."

"What do you know about my wife?" the minister cried impatiently.

"Aye. I was heading to the loch the day she disappeared. Two men rushed at her from those trees." He pointed in the direction of a copse of firs. "They gagged her and took her on a boat."

"Do you know who they were?" Dr. Mac asked.

"One was that tourism official, Barbour."

"Are you sure?" Lindsey asked.

"Aye, lass. He's been slinking around here a lot. Trying to promote his monster so the area will modernize. Him and that foolish reporter Campbell. Can't leave well enough alone. Which is why I tried to scare you off when you came here, Reverend. I wanted the loch to stay as it is. I'm terribly sorry now. Besides, I stopped pulling pranks after those fellows came along, the ones who took your wife."

"I see." Dr. Mac paused, then asked, "Was Campbell the other man with Barbour?"

"Aye."

Dr. Mac pulled at his hair. "Do you know where they took my wife?"

"She went with them on their boat."

"What kind of boat?"

"A fancy thing," he said. "It looked new."

Dr. Mac became quiet as the others plied the Highlander with their own questions. Finally he said, "At the police station I overheard Will Campbell say his newspaper was giving him a new boat for his monster story."

"I'll bet that's the connection!" Lindsey cried.

"Would you like to come with us?" Dr. Mac asked the strange, hulking man.

He shook his head. "I've had enough of people for one day." He paused. "I do hope you find your wife."

They all thanked the Highlander, and he disappeared like a ghost into the misty moors.

Dr. Mac then locked Burnsey inside the croft . "Let's go," he said.

Chapter Fourteen

Lindsey shivered in the cool night air, watching in fascination as fog elves pitched about the darkened loch. Sometimes they collided with the prince's boat, breaking up like mist from a boiling pot. Above them stars twinkled lazily, visible in stops and starts.

They passed two small boats manned by diehard Highland fisherman out to get a good catch for the market. Kerosene lanterns provided their only light.

Dr. Mac guided the boat quietly through the dark water, keeping the lights down so they didn't scare the elusive Nessie, should the creature be around. The boys and T.J. kept him company in the posh cabin with its white leather seats decorated with the Prince of Wales's crest. Well, the boys did anyway. T.J. had fallen asleep.

No one spoke, as Dr. Kerr said she didn't want any unnecessary noises to scare Nessie away. Lindsey watched the professor as she slowly stalked around the boat, scanning the waters with high-powered binoculars. She reminded Lindsey of Burnsey with his ears darted straight up, on the alert, ready to pounce or bark. Which was exactly why he hadn't made the trip. As they had prepared to leave the croft, Sarah had volunteered to stay behind with the Westie. But T.J. wouldn't permit it. Later, Lindsey had told Sarah privately, "He wants us to be ready to go home. We all need to be together for that to happen."

Lindsey watched now as they hummed over the face of the water. Dr. Mac searched through the mists with his own binoculars as he steered the boat. She wondered what he must be going through. His courage and calmness inspired her.

"Lindsey?" Sarah, sitting next to her, interrupted her thoughts.

"Uh-huh?"

"I just wanted to say I'm sorry for the times I made fun of your faith."

Lindsey turned to her, astonished. "Well, thanks. What brought that on?"

"I've been watching Dr. Mac through all of this. He's upset and stuff, but he's also really sure that God has everything under control." She shook her head. "That's amazing. Most people would be losing their minds about now." She sighed. "I'm a little embarrassed that all I've thought about is getting rich and famous off this experience."

"So that's not important to you anymore?"

Sarah shook her head. "Nah. And you know what else?"

"What?"

"Whether or not Dr. Kerr gets her pictures tonight—or any night after this—doesn't matter. She said she believes in an eel-like Nessie, and that's good enough for me, just like Dr. Mac and y'all believe in God, and how I've started to these past few days."

Lindsey was excited, but she kept her voice down. "That's some discovery, Sarah! I'm really happy you're thinking this way."

"Have you been through any really hard times?"

"Well, it was pretty terrible when my Uncle Mark died in

that accident. For a few months I didn't even want to get into a car."

"Did your faith help you?" Sarah asked.

"Oh, yes!" Lindsey exclaimed in a whisper. "God really comforted me. And then there was knowing that because Uncle Mark loved Jesus, I knew I'd see him again some day in heaven."

"That must be nice." Sarah sighed. She stared at her hands, resting in her lap.

"It is, Sarah. But it's not just for me or Dr. Mac, you know. God loves you, too. He wants you to love him and his Son, Jesus." This wasn't nearly as difficult as she had feared it would be. It seemed natural for Lindsey to tell Sarah what Jesus meant to her—and what he could mean to Sarah.

"Is that it? It seems like it should be harder than that."

"Not really. Not for us, anyway. Our sins separate us from God. Someone had to pay the price for them and lead us back to God. Jesus did that on the cross. If you believe that and accept what he did, you can know God, too."

"I'd like that."

"Would it be okay if I led you through a prayer?" Lindsey suggested nervously.

"I guess. If you think it's important."

"I do. Repeat after me. 'Lord Jesus, I love you, and I want you to forgive my sins and live in my heart. Thank you for dying so that I can live with God forever.'"

Sarah repeated the words, and just as the two girls hugged, the professor became very agitated.

"I see it," Dr. Kerr cried in a fierce whisper. "There's your monster!" She started snapping pictures, the ones that would show the world the truth about Nessie.

Lindsey and Sarah rushed to her side on their soft-soled boat shoes. "Where?" Lindsey asked in a hushed whisper. Her heart throbbed in her chest.

"Right—there." Dr. Kerr pointed her camera toward the water near the stern. "Tell Guthrie to stop the boat."

"I will." Sarah rushed into the cabin to relay the message.

"I see it, Dr. Kerr!" Lindsey cried, forgetting to whisper. "It's so big!"

The professor took several pictures as the slithery creature came up and went back down, rhythmically, like a song.

"See those bumps," Lindsey said, pointing. "What are they?"

Sarah returned with the boys, and they all stared in fascination at the creature.

"I see it, too," Ben said. He sounded happy for the first time since he'd come on the adventure.

"It's more incredible than anything I've imagined. How big do you think it is?" Lindsey asked.

Dr. Kerr guessed about twenty feet long.

"It really is eel-like," Lindsey said. "Are you getting good pictures?"

"So good I can hardly believe it." The professor crept slowly along the side of the boat, following the animal's movements.

"A-are we in danger?" Sarah asked.

"No, it won't hurt you," the professor assured them. "Just keep your voices down so we don't scare old Nessie."

"Is there more than one?" Lindsey asked.

"I can't tell. I'm only seeing one right now, but there could be another in the area. I can't believe my good luck."

"It's way more than that," Sarah said.

Suddenly, out of the mists, another boat appeared, heading right toward their vessel! With a loud crash, the other boat collided with them.

Sarah grabbed Lindsey, keeping her from pitching into the water. Dr. Mac tossed in his seat like Captain Kirk in *Star Trek*. Dr. Kerr and the boys grabbed hand railings and held on for dear life. Once she recovered her balance, Lindsey saw that T.J. had slept through the whole thing! They must be getting close to leaving Loch Ness if T.J. could sleep through such a commotion.

Boom! Another smack into the prince's boat sent Lindsey sprawling on the deck. She seized a mast and clung to it as Sarah slid past, clutched Lindsey's leg, and hung on.

"Not my camera!" Dr. Kerr wailed as it jerked loose from her hands and splashed into the unforgiving waters of Loch Ness. "My life's work!"

Then Lindsey heard a woman's voice yelling at them from the other boat. "Mrs. Mac!" she cried out.

Dr. Mac burst from the cabin when he heard Lindsey's exclamation. Suddenly his wife appeared on the other boat, the fog swirling around her like a skirt. "Guthrie!" she hollered.

Lindsey sat up carefully, trying to avoid a large piece of splintered boat. Mrs. Mac was waving her arms wildly to attract their attention. Something that looked like an unfastened rope hung from one of her wrists. Lindsey could see Nessie lurking in the background, as if in wait for a late night snack. What if the legendary monster really was just that, a monster? What if one of them fell overboard? What would Nessie do?

"Mary!" Dr. Mac suddenly leaped from the prince's boat to the other one.

Just then David Barbour, the tourism official, grabbed Mrs. Mac. He kicked at the pastor, who struggled to stay upright on the rocking deck. Dr. Mac went down hard, but he got right back up again. Lindsey strained to hear and see what was going on.

"Stay away from my wife!" he cried.

"Somebody get T.J. to take the wheel!" Dr. Kerr ordered.

Lindsey slipped and slid her way to the cabin, where T.J. was groggily rousing himself.

"What's going on?" he asked.

There wasn't time to explain. To Lindsey's horror, the other boat was headed straight for them again. She grabbed the wheel and cranked it to the left, but not fast enough. The third jolt knocked everyone to the deck. She and T.J. spurted out of the cabin like toothpaste under pressure. She watched as T.J. slid hard and fast head-first into a gear box, which seemed to knock him unconscious. He continued to slide across the deck and would have gone overboard, but Lindsey quickly reached out and grabbed his foot. Sarah held her steady. Lindsey wasn't about to let Nessie eat T.J.

"Hold on!" Dr. Kerr yelled at the girls, as she clung to a mast.

As she tugged on T.J.'s foot, Lindsey saw Dr. Mac still fighting David Barbour, who had now thrown Mrs. Mac to the deck. Suddenly the other boat's skipper—Will Campbell, the reporter—appeared and grasped one of T.J.'s arms. He yanked hard, trying to pull the teacher into the water that separated the two boats.

"You thought you could best us!" he screamed.

"Ben! Andrew!" Lindsey roared above the noises. They couldn't let go of T.J.

"Help!" Sarah cried.

Ben and Andrew rushed to their rescue and helped the girls hold onto T.J. However, the full weight of the boat as it started to drift was against them. Inch by inch, T.J. slipped closer to the water as the distance between the boats yawned open.

"Oh, God, please help us!" Sarah screamed into the night.

And he did. Just as the teacher was about to slip into the dark waters, to be attacked by Nessie or rammed by the other boat, Lindsey's hands grew hot. Then her feet went all pins and needles.

"What's this?" Sarah cried. "I'm going numb."

"Hold on!" the boys cheered. "Don't let go whatever you do!"

Lindsey felt herself sliding down, down, down, not to the waters but to another time, another place. Just before darkness closed in on them, Lindsey saw the outlines of two Loch Ness creatures watching curiously in the safe distance.

"It's time to get off, y'all," the frizzy-haired Nauticus employee told the Dreamers as they sat, slightly dazed, in the pod. "You've already been on the virtual reality ride twice."

"Ah…" T.J. stretched his long legs. "I guess we'd better go."

"Look at that line." The girl shook her head. Her earrings jingled, as if they were irritated, too.

Lindsey was the first one out of the pod. Her legs ached, and her mind reeled. Sarah, bleary-eyed and stunned, practically crawled out after her. Ben and Andrew climbed creakily from the ride, reaching back in to pull T.J. to freedom.

"That must have been some ride!" Ben's mother said as she saw their bedraggled appearances.

"It certainly was!" Lindsey's right hand ached, but she was glad to be home again, safe and sound.

"Look what I found while you were in the ride." Aunt Mary Ann produced a small booklet she had purchased at a souvenir stand.

"Well, look at this!" Ben said as he examined it. He began to read aloud, "Although there has been no absolute proof of Nessie's existence, paleontologist Margaret Kerr, along with the Reverend Dr. Guthrie MacRae and his wife, spotted what they claimed to be the Loch Ness Monster in the 1930s. They also exposed a hoax created by a Scottish journalist and a tourism official."

"How about that!" Lindsey was beside herself. "I'm so glad to know what happened to them."

Mrs. Tyler looked confused. "You know these people?" she asked, wide-eyed.

"Oh sure," Lindsey said in a Scottish accent, then whispered to Sarah, "Our secret, right?"

Sarah nodded. "Fame, money, who needs it?" She looked at Lindsey. "I guess there are some things that are more important."

Lindsey just smiled.